A HISTORY OF
FIREFIGHTING IN
CAMBRIDGESHIRE

A HISTORY OF FIREFIGHTING IN CAMBRIDGESHIRE

EDDIE BAKER

JEREMY MILLS

PUBLISHING

Published by Jeremy Mills Publishing Limited
The Red House, 22 Occupation Road, Lindley, Huddersfield HD3 3BD
www.jeremymillspublishing.co.uk

First Published 2006
© Eddie Baker 2006

ISBN 1-905217-10-2

A CIP catalogue record for this book is available from the British Library

Typeset in Monotype Bembo and Gill Sans Extra Bold by Concept, Huddersfield
Printed by Replika Press Pt. Ltd

CONTENTS

THE AUTHOR

EDDIE BAKER's life in the fire service started in 1960 in his native Croydon when he joined the Croydon Auxiliary Fire Service. Eddie was promoted through the ranks to Sub Officer prior to the time of amalgamation with the London Fire Brigade in 1965. He continued to serve in the AFS until disbandment in 1968. By 1970 Eddie had moved home and joined the Cambridgeshire and Isle of Ely Fire Brigade and was stationed in Gamlingay. After local government re-organisation in 1974 he served with the Cambridge-shire Fire and Rescue Service and transferred to St Neots Fire Station in 1977 before retiring in 1995 as a Leading Firefighter.

Married to Ann they have a son Mark, a daughter Lisa and three grand-daughters, Lauren, Siobhan and Hannah.

This is Eddie's second book, his first *On the Run – A History of Croydon Fire Brigade* was published in 2004. He has also written a number of articles which have been published in Fire Service related magazines.

ACKNOWLEDGEMENTS

I MUST firstly acknowledge the assistance given to me by the Cambridgeshire Fire and Rescue Service without which this book would never have been written. From the very beginning the Chief Fire Officer, Tom Carroll, Q.F.S.M., M.I.Fire E., has given his full support for the project and has been backed up by many others in both headquarters and around the stations. In particular I must give special thanks to ADO Andy Dunlop for his information on New Dimensions, Graham Wiggins the Fleet & Equipment Manager, Danny Rust the Estates and Property Manager, Hayley Buzzell and her predecessor Neil Thompson in the Publicity and Press Office and to Tony de Matteis of the Peterborough Volunteer Fire Brigade.

My gratitude also goes to the following retired members; ADO Tony Brotchie, Sub O. Gordon Townsend and Sub O. Gordon Depledge for access to their photographic and other records. The following members of The Fire Brigade Society have also supplied photographs for inclusion in the book; David Palmer, Geoffrey Heathcock, George Dunlop, Karl Sillitoe, Mike Sudds and Peter Ashpool. Keith Wardell also provided photographs from his excellent collection. Then my thanks must go to the staff at the County Record Offices at Cambridge and Huntingdon for their help in accessing their many historical records. The Cambridgeshire Libraries, who hold the archives of the *Cambridge Evening News, Hunts. Post* and *Wisbech Standard* newspapers, are thanked for their help and also the *Peterborough Evening Telegraph*. I also give thanks to Lewis Summer and to The Fire Brigade Society for the supply of historical fleet lists.

To Jeremy Mills, my publisher, I give a special thank you for his professionalism in supporting this project and his work in the design and layout of the book. Lastly, but not least I must praise my wife, Ann, for not only putting up with me shut away for many hours working on this book but for her assistance in helping me with my research in reading through mounds of old records.

Eddie Baker
Alconbury, 2006

FOREWORD

IT is a particular pleasure for me to welcome this book and to introduce you to a history of the selfless public service afforded by local firefighters. A Service too often taken for granted and exceptional in that firefighters put their own lives at risk in saving the lives and property of others.

As a former Cambridgeshire firefighter, Eddie Baker is well qualified to tell the story of firefighting in Cambridgeshire. This book, apart from being informative, pays a long overdue tribute to the work of the Fire & Rescue Service in this County. A tribute to the men and women who watch and wait, 24 hours of every day, of every month, of every year, ready to deal with the unknown dangers that accident, malice and envy can bring to others and to themselves.

This is a well illustrated historical record of a service that has evolved from the village volunteers of pre-war years, via a number of local government re-organisations, into the modern service that the County of Cambridgeshire and City of Peterborough and its citizens can be very proud. As well as appealing to serving and retired firefighters, this book will surely be enjoyed by ordinary readers who simply want to know something more about the Fire and Rescue Service. It may also leave the reader asking for more and I hope Eddie is able to provide just that in the future.

Tom Carroll, Q.F.S.M., M.I.Fire E.
Chief Fire Officer, Cambridgeshire Fire & Rescue Service

THE FIREMAN

I WOULD like to suggest he is 'the person next door', he is a 'man's man' with a sharp memory and a 'little boy' who never got over the excitement of engines and sirens and smoke and danger. He is a person like you and me with warts and worries and unfulfilled dreams, yet he stands taller than most of us. He is a fireman, he puts it all 'out on the line' when the bell rings. The fireman is at once the most fortunate and least fortunate of men; he is a man who savours life because he has seen too much death. He is a gentle man because he has seen too much of the awesome power of the violent forces out of control, he is a man responsive to a child's laughter because his arms have held too many small bodies who will never laugh again. He is a man who appreciates the simple pleasures of life – hot coffee held in numbed, unbending fingers; the flush of fresh air pumping through smoke and fire convulsed lungs; a warm bed for bone and muscle compelled beyond feeling; the camaraderie of brave men; the divine peace of selfless service; and a job well done in the name of all men.

He does not wear buttons or wave flags or shout obscenities and when he marches it is to honour a fallen comrade – he does not preach the brotherhood of man, he lives it.

J. C. Maxwell, O.B.E., D.F.C. (Bar), Q.F.S.M.
Chief Fire Officer 1974–1978

Previously published in *A History of the Huntingdonshire and Peterborough County Fire Service 1965–1974.*

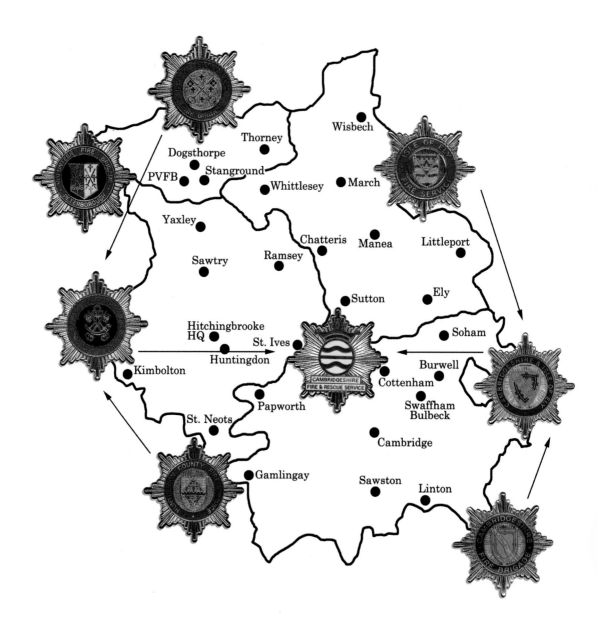

THE BADGE

THE badge of the Cambridgeshire Fire and Rescue Service crest was the first one in the British Fire Services to incorporate the word 'Rescue' in its title. Over the intervening years other brigades have followed suit.

The crown represents the dioceses of Ely, Northampton and Peterborough. On the badge itself the wavy lines denote the Rivers Ouse and Nene and the straight line the Fens, all sources of prosperity and development for the County.

INTRODUCTION

FIREFIGHTING in Great Britain first originated in Roman times when the *Corps of Vigiles* was established. By today's standards their functions were very basic, e.g. the use of long hooks for pulling down buildings in the path of fires and the forming of bucket chains. With the fall of the Roman Empire organised firefighting rapidly fell into decline until around the time of the Great Fire of London in 1666.

Following this disastrous fire, insurance companies began to establish their own fire brigades during the latter part of the seventeenth century. Originally these brigades, each clad in different colourful uniforms, only attended fires in premises insured with them which had plaques, known as Fire Marks, attached to the outside wall to indicate which company they were insured with. Some of these firemarks are still in existence today although their need has long passed into distant history.

The pump pictured on the following page is typical of the early manual fire engines in that it had to be manhandled to the scene of the fire and then the handles on the sides pumped up and down to produce a jet of water. The water itself was supplied by a bucket chain and was tipped into the cistern of the pump.

Firemen of the Sun Insurance and Cornhill Insurance Brigades

Sun Insurance Fire Mark, Cathedral Precincts Peterborough (photo – Gordon Townsend Collection)

Swaffham Prior's 1791 Manual Fire Engine (photo – Tony Brotchie collection)

In the meantime many of the large cities had formed their own municipal brigades; in London, for example, the grouping of the larger insurance brigades was formed in 1833 into the London Fire Engine Establishment, later to become the Metropolitan Fire Brigade and eventually to be renamed the London Fire Brigade. Other cities formed Police Fire Brigades where selected officers performed the duties of firemen. However, the majority of the country was served by part time men paid a turn-out fee or those giving free voluntary service.

Prior to 1938 the area covered by this book, namely that now served by the Cambridgeshire Fire and Rescue Service, had a hotchpotch of systems where the City of Cambridge had a police fire brigade, Peterborough had two different brigades; the City Fire Brigade which was run by the City Council and the Peterborough Volunteer Fire Brigade. The remainder of the towns and villages were served by retained brigades, employed by local councils, and volunteer brigades.

This variety of systems continued until the Fire Brigades Act of 1938 when legislation was passed which required all local councils throughout Great Britain to provide firefighting services for the areas under their control. Where some of these councils were too small to run their own Fire Brigade, neighbouring councils were paid to provide the necessary service or they formed joint brigades.

At this time there were some 1,600 different fire brigades of varying sizes and efficiency serving Great Britain. Under the threat of war the Auxiliary Fire Service was created and soon volunteers had been enrolled to undertake the necessary training. In 1939 the Second World War was declared and the country suffered from the heavy air raids of 1940 and 1941. Many problems were caused by these air raids in such matters as procedures, training, organisation, appliances and equipment in use by the many different brigades which together attended these large infernos. Consequently, in August 1941, as a war-time measure, the National Fire Service was formed by amalgamating all of the local brigades and the Auxiliary Fire Service into one single organisation and officer rankings, appliances and equipment were standardised across the country.

With the cessation of hostilities, local authorities were soon requesting that the control of the fire service was returned to their control. However, it was not until 1947 that the Fire Services Act was passed by parliament and on the 1st April 1948 the Fire Service was de-nationalised and returned to local authority control, however, this time there were now only 146 brigades under City, County or County Borough control. At the current time, due to various other local government changes, the number of fire brigades serving the UK has been reduced to fifty-eight.

In 1948 this area was served by four County Brigades, namely Cambridgeshire Fire Brigade with ten fire stations, Huntingdon County Fire Service with seven fire stations, Isle of Ely Fire Service with nine fire stations and the Soke of Peterborough Fire Brigade with just the one fire station. There was also the

Peterborough Volunteer Fire Brigade (PVFB) with its fire station in the city centre.

Following further Local Government re-organisations in 1965 and 1974, all four brigades were eventually amalgamated into one large Fire Authority. In an innovative move the new Chief Fire Officer John Maxwell, D.F.C. (Bar) created the first British Fire Service to include the word 'Rescue' into its title.

It is now over 30 years since the inception of the Cambridgeshire Fire and Rescue Service and the role of the service is continually evolving. Following the terrible events in the United States of America on September 11th 2001 the British Government instigated a £350 million New Dimension Programme that defined the role of the Fire and Rescue Services in the event of catastrophic events on a local, regional or national scale including terrorist attacks, chemical, biological, radiological or nuclear incidents, search and rescue from trapped situations and major flooding incidents. It drew into the Office of the Deputy Prime Minister (ODPM) the expertise of over 100 specialist officers to bring together what had been a localised Fire & Rescue Service into one that could work across County and regional boundaries in a more organised and effective manner.

To deal with these various risks and tasks, central government has funded the design and equipped a number of new appliances each with specific roles or capabilities. These include the Incident Response Unit (IRU) carrying equipment capable of the mass decontamination of up to 400 people per hour. These appliances also carry equipment for the use of firefighters such as gas tight suits, detection and monitoring equipment. The eighty IRUs have been located on a risk-assessed basis with at least one located to each of the Fire and Rescue Services. The Urban Search and Rescue Teams (USAR), nineteen in all and allocated regionally, are for use in the event of industrial and domestic accidents or building collapse and each team comprises six individual pod units, three prime movers and an on-call team of thirty specialist firefighters plus two search dogs. To deal with major flooding incidents, where there are serious threats to human life and welfare, a High Volume Pump Unit (HVPU) has been designed to be capable of pumping a maximum of 8,000 litres per minutes, as against the 2,250 litres per minute of a standard fire appliance. These fifty appliances have a hose laying and retrieval system capable of putting down 3 km of 150 mm delivery hose and can lift water from 60 metres as opposed to the normal 8 metres.

Already in use, IRUs have been mobilised to various incidents around the country. In 2004 a serious building collapse in Glasgow drew USAR units from as far south as London. In 2005 Carlisle suffered serious flooding and eight HVPUs were sent from training duties at the Fire Service College to assist with the dispersal of floodwaters. Also in late 2005 following the explosion at the Buncefield Oil Depot, twenty-eight HVPUs were mobilised to lay 42 km of hose to supply the large quantities of water required to extinguish the flames.

Aerial Rescue Pump (photo – the Author's collection)

Still to come are the Mass Decontamination Resilience Units, an enhanced detection and monitoring capability, large capacity boat facilities and the equipment to deal with large scale floods on the scale of the 1953 East Coast disaster. The final part of the New Dimension project is likely to be a number of mobile command and control village facilities.

What else does the future hold for the Fire and Rescue Service? The ODPM has decreed that the forty-six English Control Centres, currently run by each individual brigade, are to be amalgamated into nine Regional Controls, with the

Turntable Ladder Pump (photo – Ralph Horton with acknowledgements to GB Fire Ltd)

Eastern Regional Control Centre to be built in Waterbeach by 2009. Also brigades are combining together as purchasing consortiums for the supply of appliances and uniforms. Is this the thin edge of the wedge and will we soon have Regional Fire and Rescue Services or even a National Fire and Rescue Service? Time will tell.

New appliances are being designed and built, some with multi-role applications for example in Scotland, Strathclyde Fire & Rescue Service have had built an Aerial Rescue Pump with a boom and rescue cage that can extend to 28.5 metres. As well as a range of extension ladders it also carries full firefighting kit, hydraulic rescue equipment, 1,500 litres of water and 125 litres of foam. In England, Buckinghamshire has had a similar appliance built but this time with a turntable ladder mounted onto a pumping appliance.

Regardless of any changes in the future the men and women carrying out firefighting in this County will continue to serve with the same dedication and professionalism of the past and this book is dedicated to the firefighters of Cambridgeshire past, present and future.

Eddie Baker
Alconbury, 2006

PART ONE

PRE-SECOND WORLD WAR

IT should be noted that this chapter is not a definitive list of every local fire brigade in the area, but is intended to show the reader how the fire service evolved from the 17th century up to the declaration of war in 1939.

Cambridge

Although there are records of fires in Cambridge as far back as 1174 it was not until the 16th century that there was any form of organised firefighting in the city when there was an issue of buckets and ladders to the various colleges and churches.

The Cambridge Volunteer Fire Brigade was formed in 1875 and used hose carts and ladders distributed around some seven stations in the town. Gradually more equipment was added and in 1909 a horse drawn steam fire engine was acquired. A Volunteer Fire Brigade was also formed in Chesterton but this was amalgamated with the Cambridge Brigade in 1911.

In 1921, the Cambridge Borough Police Fire Brigade was created and took over the responsibility of fire defence in Cambridge, operating a motor pump

Dennis Pump CE 7352 of the Cambridge Borough Police Fire Brigade (photo – Tony Brotchie collection)

Leyland FK8A Pump DVE 600 – new to Cambridge Borough Police Fire Brigade in 1938
(photo – Tony Brotchie collection)

and a motor escape carrier. The combined Police and Fire Station in St Andrews Street is still standing but is now used for other purposes. The Chief Constable was nominally the Chief Fire Officer and the brigade consisted of six constables under a sergeant. When the Air Raid Precautions Act was passed in 1938 an additional six constables were employed to assist with training the newly formed Auxiliary Fire Service.

Chatteris
In the early days the Chatteris District Local Board was operating two Horse Drawn Manual Fire Engines. Later taken over by the Chatteris Urban District Council it then operated a Dennis Motor Fire Pump, originally with solid tyres, but later adapted to pneumatic tyres.

Ely
The local Board of Health maintained a firefighting organisation of sorts during the middle of the 19th century, until this was replaced by a volunteer fire brigade in 1877. The old Fire Engine House on St Mary's Green housed two manual pumps and an escape was kept in the old Holy Trinity Bell Tower in the High Street. The volunteer fire brigade appeared to have faded away in the 1880s when a new brigade was formed by the local council, under the control of the Council Surveyor. This lasted until 1904 when a Colonel Archer took over and re-arranged the siting of the equipment for greater convenience.

Chatteris U.D.C. Fire Brigade's Dennis Pump (photo – Gordon Townsend collection)

One of the two Manual Pumps used by Ely U.D.C. Fire Brigade, 1912
(photo – Gordon Townsend collection)

Ely U.D.C. Shand Mason Steamer (photo – Gordon Townsend collection)

In 1912 the manufacturers Shand Mason offered £20 against the part exchange of one of the manual fire engines for a Steam Fire Engine. To house this new engine the council built a more modern fire station complete with a hose drying tower. Originally pulled by two horses from the *Bell Hotel*, the steamer was later adapted to be pulled by a lorry. Eventually it was put onto a chassis fitted with pneumatic tyres to make it easier to tow. It can now be seen in the Ely Fire Station Museum.

Huntingdon

The first Engine House was built in the early 18th century in the High Street, opposite what is now Chequers Court, where a manual fire engine was kept. The key was originally held in the Police Station at the far end of the High Street but was later transferred to the brewery gatehouse opposite the Fire Station. In 1767 the town acquired the very latest thing in fire engines, built by Bristow of London at a cost of £64 10s (£64.50p).

In the early part of the 20th century the Chief Fire Officer of Huntingdon Borough Fire Brigade was a Captain Figg and the equipment included a horse pulled Merryweather manual pump, a wheeled fire escape ladder, a hand pulled hose cart and an ambulance. The firemen carried out ambulance duties as early as the beginning of the 20th century.

In 1909 a horse drawn steamer was purchased, which has since been lovingly restored and handed over to the Fire Service Technical College at Moreton-in-Marsh where it can be seen on display. By 1930 the brigade was operating from a

Fire Station in nearby Princes Street, the former Butchers' Market, and became motorised when Captain Gerald Barber was the proud recipient of a new Dennis Motor Fire Pump. Gerald Barber had a long association with the brigade, for as a teenager he became a call boy responsible for cycling round to alert firemen when they were needed. Later he joined as a fireman, serving under Chief Officer Figg, and rising to the rank of Chief Officer, a position he held until his retirement in 1940.

Messrs Hearn, Goodlife, and Thackray, Huntingdon Fire Brigade, 1891
(photo – Huntingdon County Record Office)

Huntingdon Borough Fire Brigade in the early 1900s (photo – Gordon Townsend collection)

Dedication ceremony of new Steam Fire Engine 1909 (photo – Huntingdon County Record Office)

Dennis Motor Fire Pump EW 6681 (photo – Pete Ashpool collection)

Huntingdon crew with various competition trophies won in 1936, (left to right) Fm. L. Cobb, Fm. C. Woodruffe, Engineer C. Howard, Chief Officer Barber, Second Engineer G. Elphick, and Fm. L. Baum (photo – Huntingdon County Record Office)

Kimbolton

The first record of a fire brigade in the village was in 1763 and there is also a record of correspondence, in 1842, between the churchwardens of Kimbolton Parish Church and a number of insurance companies confirming that they would each pay a proportion of the brigade's expenses. It is also noted that a 16 man manual fire engine was purchased in 1880 and stationed in Thrapston Road. From 1899 right through to the time of the National Fire Service, Canon Powys Maurice was the driving force of the volunteer brigade. In 1921 the station was moved to Maltings Lane and again in 1939 to Rookery Lane.

Littleport

Littleport Fire Brigade had a Merryweather Steam Fire Pump, originally pulled by a horse but later fitted with pneumatic tyres and adapted to be pulled by a lorry.

Manea

In 1830 a committee was formed to raise money to purchase a Manual Fire Engine for the village and local area. Eventually sixteen years later a Tilley Fire Engine and leather buckets were purchased for £140. Little more is known

Littleport's Merryweather Steam Fire Pump (photo – Gordon Townsend collection)

Littleport's Steamer pumping out flooded shops 1912 (photo – Gordon Depledge collection)

Manea's 1846 Tilley horse drawn Manual Fire Engine (photo – Tony Brotchie collection)

about firefighting in Manea until the 1930s when a Captain Murfitt was Chief Fire Officer who was followed by Captain Whetstone. The Fire Engine was restored in the 1960s and was on show in the foyer of Cambridge Fire Station for many years. It has now been returned to Manea and is currently being stored in the Fire Station.

March

In the late 1800s March Fire Brigade were running two horse drawn appliances; one a manual pump and the other a steam pump. In the picture below the hand draw bar seen on the steamer was used to pull the engine out of the station whilst waiting for the horses to arrive. In 1886 the steamer was transported by train to Peterborough to help in fighting a large fire in a timber yard.

Old Fletton

In the 1930s Old Fletton Urban District Council Fire Brigade, on the outskirts of Peterborough, operated a solid tyred Dennis Pump which had replaced an earlier horse drawn steamer. Their Chief Fire Officer at the time was Mr Jack Kelham and the Fire Station was in the High Street. By the mid 1930s the tyres were changed to the pneumatic type and the appliance served throughout the time of the NFS and attended fires as far afield as Liverpool.

March Fire Brigade in the late 1800s (photo – Gordon Townsend collection)

Dennis Pump of Old Fletton U.D.C. Fire Brigade (photo – Gordon Townsend collection)

Peterborough

Peterborough Fire Brigade had its origins in the 1840s when it was responsible to the Local Commissioners. Prior to this there had been some notable fires; in 1583 twenty houses were destroyed in Westgate, in 1656 thirty houses in Bridge Street and in 1835 seventy cottages were damaged or destroyed between Milton Street and Westgate making about 200 poor people homeless.

On the 9th May 1884 a disastrous fire occurred when the roof of the Peterborough Infirmary was found to be on fire. The first hose to get to work was by the Great Northern Railway Company, whose land lay to the west of the Infirmary. This was connected to a hydrant in their yard and the hose was thrown over a wall into the grounds of the Infirmary. The GNR followed this up with their manual fire engine. The Peterborough Fire Brigade had arrived soon after the first hose was got to work but wasted valuable time as they were unable to find the hydrants. The fire was eventually extinguished after about four hours. There was severe criticism in local newspapers, in the way the brigade was organised with the lack of uniforms, authority and discipline. By November of 1884 the brigade had been disbanded and was replaced by the Peterborough City Fire Brigade, responsible to the newly formed City Council. The senior officer of the new brigade was John Charles Gill and it was under the control of the Council's Waterworks Committee. In 1884 the Peterborough Volunteer Fire Brigade (PVFB) had been formed and their history is recorded in a separate chapter of this book. By 1893 the City Fire Brigade had obtained its

Peterborough City Fire Brigade in the 1920s (photo – Peterborough Volunteer Fire Brigade)

first steam fire engine and in 1923 acquired a Ford Model T pump followed in 1931 by a Dennis Self-Propelled Motor Fire Engine. In 1920 the brigade had moved into new premises in Queen Street; a building which had previously been used by the Electricity Undertaking.

Queen Street Fire Station, Peterborough, 1920 (photo – Gordon Townsend collection)

Peterborough's Dennis Big 4 Pump Escape, 1931 (photo – Gordon Townsend collection)

Ramsey

Ramsey Fire Brigade, under Chief Fire Officer Leonard Greig, was one the first brigades in Huntingdonshire to purchase a steam fire pump in 1876. However, by the mid 1930s Ramsey has been completely motorised. A motor tender had been purchased in 1934 to pull the steam pump. They were also running a self propelled Morris Commercial Pump. The Chief Fire Officer by this time was Mr George Shearer.

Ramsey's steamer seen here in a town parade (photo – Gordon Townsend collection)

Ramsey U.D.C. Fire Brigade in the 1930s (photo – Gordon Townsend collection)

Sawtry

There are records of a volunteer unit in Sawtry in 1844 operating a Manual Fire Pump, which was used in the village by a Volunteer Fire Brigade for nearly a hundred years until an AFS unit was formed at the beginning of the Second World War. Following de-nationalisation in 1948 a retained unit was set up to replace the volunteers who had served the village for so long.

Sawtry's 1844 Manual Pump pictured in 1939 (photo – Huntingdon County Record Office)

St Ives

In 1929 the Fire Station of the St Ives Borough Fire Brigade was in White Hart Lane and in the same year the Borough Council bought a Dennis Motor Pump at a cost of £1,200 which was delivered in 1930. However because it was too

Dennis Pump of St Ives Borough Fire Brigade (photo – Gordon Townsend collection)

St Ives Fire Station, East Street (photo – Pete Ashpool)

large to fit into the Fire Station it had to be kept in temporary accommodation in Market Hill until a new station was built in Station Road. Yet another move saw the brigade relocate to East Street.

St Neots

There are indications that there had been a fire brigade in St Neots as far back as 1721 when records show that a fire engine was kept in the Parish Church, thus accounting for the larger doors at the west end. Before the installation of a fire alarm siren at a local mill, the church bells were also used to call out the volunteer fire brigade. For this purpose the bells were 'rung backwards'. That is starting with the smallest and finishing with the largest.

The first recorded fire station was in New Street, originally called New Lane, which had been widened in 1843. The Local Commissioners now planned an ambitious scheme for the use of some of the surplus land. It was decided to build a fire engine house and other store rooms on the ground floor with a public room above and by 1846 the station was in use. The appliance room doors can still be seen as part of Ottakars Bookshop. In 1863 after a new Police Station had been built in New Street, the old 'Lockup' became available and was converted into a Fire Station (the site is now No. 14 High Street).

St Neots Volunteer Fire Station, Eynesbury – note call-boy centre rear
(photo – Gordon Depledge collection)

Armband as worn by the St Neots call-boys (photo – the Author)

In 1880 the St Neots Volunteer Fire Brigade moved yet again, this time to Eynesbury, just across the bridge in St Mary's Street, in the Council Depot at the rear of the *Dog & Duck* Public House. Their equipment included three horse drawn appliances; a steam fire engine, an eleven person per side Manual Pump and a four person per side Manual Pump. In January 1913 the name of the brigade changed with the word 'Volunteer' being dropped.

During the First World War there were no incidents recorded as being caused by enemy action, although the brigade did get called to Yelling Aerodrome on the 14th June 1917. No information is available regarding the incident except that the brigade's expenses came to £15. 8s. 6d. (£15.42½p). The minutes of the

St Neots Volunteer Fire Brigade seen here at a Gala Day display in Priory Park
(photo – Gordon Townsend collection)

St Neots Fire Station, Huntingdon Street, the flat roofed extension was added post-war
(photo – Cambridgeshire Fire & Rescue Service)

AGM on the 17th May 1916 recorded that any member of the brigade called up would be re-instated on return from military service and in 1917 it was noted that there were 4 members serving at the front and a guinea (£1.05p) was sent to each man from the Brigade's funds.

On the 18th June 1923 at 08.25 hours there was a call to a fire in outbuildings and the Fire Station in the Council Yard. Again no information is available on the damage caused. Later in the same year, on the 30th October the first charge for hiring a lorry to pull the steam fire pump was recorded. Prior to this it was always horses that were in use.

The thought of motorising the brigade is first recorded in July 1929 when it was proposed that a Dennis type motor fire engine with a trailer pump should be investigated.

The St Neots Urban District Council took over the running of the brigade in 1930 and the name was changed to the St Neots U.D.C. Fire Brigade and in the same year a new fire station was opened in Huntingdon Street.

In October 1932 a letter was written to Merryweathers regarding the purchase of a reconditioned motor pump. However, it was not until the 3rd December 1934 that a new Dennis Ace Motor Pump was purchased and handed over to the brigade, but its first recorded turn-out was not until the 27th April 1935 when it was sent to a house fire in Croxton.

Correspondence had been received during 1937/8 regarding the Air Raid Precautions Act but a reply had been constantly deferred. Eventually a form from the Home Office was returned stating that nothing had been done. Finally, in December 1938 following yet more correspondence, the Brigade requested that the Urban District Council advertise for Auxiliary Firemen and also to order

Dennis Ace Motor Pump EW 8489 (photo – Gordon Depledge collection)

a Dennis Trailer Pump (Medium). Earlier that year, in May, the Brigade had bought a second-hand Fire Tender for £15 from the Rushden Town Fire Brigade.

In 1939 an extension at the rear of the fire station was added to provide a watchroom, toilet and space for bunks for firemen on night duty in the event of war, and September of that year saw the introduction of call bells fitted in the firemen's homes as an aid to quicker turnouts.

Captains of the St Neots Fire Brigades

F. Nichols	April 1909 to June 1911
M McNish	July 1911 to October 1911
T. L. Williamson	November 1911 to October 1930
H. Smith★	November 1930 to January 1942

★ Became a Section Leader during the time of the N.F.S. and the first post-war Sub Officer.

Thorney

The original Thorney Fire Brigade was organised by the then owner of the local estate, the Duke of Bedford and consisted of a horse drawn manual appliance and the crew were mobilised by ringing the bell on what is now the Council building in Tank Yard. When the estate was sold in 1910 the responsibility for the brigade was transferred to the Thorney Parish Council. In 1920 the brigade purchased a Shand Mason Steam Fire Engine. It was originally pulled by horses

Thorney's first Fire Station (photo – the Author)

Thorney's Shand Mason Steam Fire Engine (photo – Gordon Townsend collection)

then by a lorry belonging to a local builder. Later a second-hand motor tender was purchased from the PVFB for £10.

Whittlesey
In the early days Whittlesey Urban District Council operated a Merryweather Manual Fire Engine pulled by a horse provided by a local farmer. It was

Whittlesey Fire Station, Inhams Lane (photo – Pete Ashpool)

Whittlesey firemen taking a break during a land fire (photo – Gordon Townsend collection)

replaced by a Bedford Motor Pump which stayed in use until nationalisation when it was declared obsolete by the NFS and dumped into a local clay pit. The original Fire Station was in the Town Hall but prior to the Second World War a new station was built in Inhams Lane.

Wisbech

In the early 1800s Wisbech Borough Fire Brigade were operating three manual fire engines and an escape ladder from their Hill Street Fire Station. The brigade consisted of Superintendent James Anchor and 23 men and was considered efficient enough to protect the town. A committee from the Town Council however did inspect a number of steam fire engines and recommended the purchase of one for £650, but the Council itself did not adopt the proposal.

However, on the 7th November 1884 a large fire in Whitehead's Timber Yard took place at South Brink, Wisbech. Assistance was requested from March Fire Brigade who responded with a steam fire engine pulled by four horses, arriving in 1¼ hours.

Another serious fire occurred on New Year's morning 1885, which destroyed the ironmongery shop of Mr W. Lane. Almost immediately afterwards the Town Council met and ordered a Shand Mason Steam Fire Engine for £800 and in a ceremony on the 18th March 1885 the steamer was started by the

Hill Street Fire Station, Wisbech (photo – Gordon Townsend collection)

Leyland FT1 Pump Escape 'Vivien' EB 9734 (photo – Mike Sudds)

Mayoress, Mrs Peatling, and named 'Etty' after her. By 1900 the brigade consisted of Captain Plowright, Superintendent Blott, 27 other officers and men and operated two steamers, one manual and the escape ladder truck. In May 1920 Captain Horace Friend took over command of the brigade and commenced a programme of modernisation. A change from using horses to a lorry and two cars improved running time from 6 to 30 mph. In 1926 and 1927 two trailer pumps were purchased and these were named 'Edith' and 'Eliza' in common with the practice of naming appliances after the mayoress of the time. Both steamers were phased out, the wheels removed, placed on dredgers and used for removing mud and silt from the docks and the River Nene. The pride of Wisbech is 'Vivien', a Leyland FT1 Pump Escape EB 9734, built for the Borough of Wisbech Fire Brigade in 1932 at a cost of £1,500 and now lovingly restored by George Dunlop.

The 26th April 1933 saw the official opening of a new fire station in Horsefair, built at a cost of £4,455 and reputedly based on the headquarters of the Birmingham Fire Brigade. This was a much larger building than the Hill Street station, which was closed down and the Hosefair station remained in use until 1987. The old escape ladder was replaced in 1935 when a second-hand 85 ft. Turntable Ladder was purchased from the Birmingham Fire Brigade and named 'Vere'.

Another appliance, a Leyland Cub fully enclosed Limousine Pump, which could carry a crew of twelve, was purchased in 1938 to replace the 18 year old lorry, and was named 'Olive'. The brigade remained retained manned until 1938 when the first fulltime firemen were employed.

Yaxley crew preparing to attend a wedding with the 1924 Ford Model T Tender
(photo – Gordon Townsend collection)

Yaxley

The Fire Station in Yaxley was originally built in 1878 to house a horse drawn Manual Pump. This station is still in use today serving as the station lecture room. In 1924 the brigade, under Chief Fire Officer Ossie Richardson, had purchased a Model 'T' Ford Tender to tow a trailer pump.

In 1936, when under the control of the Norman Cross Rural District Council, the brigade then became the proud owners of a Leyland Cub FK6 Pump, which served during the Second World War and through into the days of the Huntingdonshire County Fire Service.

Incidents

1174 – Cambridge. Most of the town was destroyed by fire. The Holy Trinity Church suffered complete destruction and other churches, then built of wood, were badly damaged.

1385 – Cambridge. Another serious fire in the town destroyed more than 100 houses.

1684 – Kimbolton. The White Lion Inn was destroyed and the adjoining house badly damaged in a serious fire.

1727 – Burwell. A group of strollers on their way to Sturbridge Fair in Cambridge decided to put on a play in a barn in Burwell. For reasons unknown the door to the barn was not only locked but nailed across. Some straw caught fire and the fire soon spread causing the deaths of 72 persons, mostly children. At the time it was thought to be of accidental cause but in 1774 an old man, on his deathbed, confessed to setting fire to the barn. There is an old manuscript in the British Museum recording the facts and in Burwell churchyard can be seen the Flaming Heart gravestone in memory of the victims.

1731 – Ramsey. Most of the High Street and Great Whyte were gutted in a disastrous fire which burnt for several days.

1741 – Huntingdon. Most of St Germain Street was gutted by a fire, despite the efforts of the fire brigade who apparently drank £1 5s. 6d (£1.27½p) worth of beer in their attempts.

1743 – Huntingdon. The Old Court House was burnt out in a very serious fire.

1802 – Alconbury. A fire destroyed Martin's Farm with all its buildings and stacks as well as six cottages.

1824 – Somersham. A fire broke out in a barn which spread to twenty dwelling houses which were completely destroyed, the fire raging for over three hours. In common with many other fires, which occurred at the time in Huntingdonshire, it was believed to be the work of an arsonist. Later that year 21-year-old Thomas Savage was brought before the Assizes charged with arson. He was found guilty and sentenced to death. In December of that year he became the last person in Huntingdonshire to be executed for arson.

1839 – St Neots. The following is a contemporary record of a fire which occurred in a farm off Cambridge Street near to where Manor Farm Road now stands:

> On the 14th of January, a dreadful and alarming fire occurred at Mr Peppercorn's Farm. It was first observed by the Watchman going his rounds. Fortunately a north west gale was blowing so the house was saved, and probably the town also, but seven fine horses and twelve pigs perished. Most of the stacks were threshed out. Men worked all night with a plentiful supply of water. It is thought to have been the work of an incendiary. Next morning groups of little urchins were seen deliberately cutting off flesh from the half roasted pigs, and hungry dogs sharing in the bountiful repast which this melancholy catastrophe offered them. The remains of seven horses were thrown into the saw pit.

1849 – Cambridge. A destructive fire occurred in Market Hill which destroyed eight houses, the firefighters being able to obtain water only from the Conduit and the river at Garret Hostel Bridge. Accounts indicate that at this time there were at least ten engines in Cambridge, some operated by the police, some by insurance companies and some by colleges.

1850 – Warboys. A serious fire struck the village and despite the valiant attempts of the Ramsey and St Ives Brigades a large farmhouse and twenty-one cottages were destroyed. The homeless inhabitants were given shelter in the village church.

1863 – Huntingdon. The High Street end of the George Hotel was gutted in a fire and reconstructed, while the coaching yard and the buildings forming the rear entrance are all that remain of the fine 17th century structure.

1876 – Abbots Ripton. On the 22nd January, a few miles north of Huntingdon, Abbots Ripton was the scene of a famous train disaster. A coal train was being shunted into sidings when it was hit by the Scottish Express, which itself was in collision with a London train coming in the opposite direction. Fifteen people were killed and the crash led to radical changes in signalling methods throughout the whole of the rail network.

1891 – Peterborough. It was the practice in cold winters for the heating apparatus in the Congregational Chapel in Westgate to be started on a Saturday to heat the building ready for the Sunday service. The building was checked at midnight on the Saturday but in the early hours the alarm was raised by a passing Police Officer. The City Fire Station was close by and the brigade was quickly to work and was connected to three hydrants before word was passed to the PVFB. Their hose truck was brought to the fire and soon got to work from a

Congregational Chapel Fire, Westgate, Peterborough 1891 (photo – Peterborough Volunteer Fire Brigade)

fourth hydrant. However, the fire had gained a strong hold on the building and despite the efforts of both brigades the fire spread to the roof and woodwork of the Chapel. There was little that could be done except to stop the fire spreading to adjoining buildings. The roof quickly fell in, molten lead ran from the windows and large quantities of bricks and heavy stonework fell, narrowly missing several firemen. By daybreak the fire had virtually burnt itself out and all that remained were the four walls.

1898 – The Green, Eynesbury. When there was a report of a barn fire on Eynesbury Green a youth ran to St Neots to summon the fire brigade and found them being entertained by their Captain, Aldred Jordan, on the lawn of his house in Huntingdon Street and very reluctant to either leave, or believe in the authenticity of the fire. When at last the horse drawn manual fire engine approached, by way of Montague Street, and the horse saw the smoke and flames, it refused to go on. It then had to be driven back to the church, turned down Berkeley Street, and unhitched by the pond on the green, from which water was pumped on to the fire. By this time the barn was totally destroyed but adjoining properties were saved.

1900 – Warboys. On the 25th September, children playing with matches caused a disastrous fire which swept through the village. One fireman was killed and fifty people were made homeless.

1903 – St Neots. Nutters Flour Mill in Bedford Street was destroyed by a fire with damage estimated at £15,000.

1905 – St Neots. Paines Brewery and Flour Mill in the Market Square were destroyed in yet another mill fire. Fortunately another nearby mill was vacant and was at once purchased and milling restarted within a few days, the former premises being rebuilt purely as a brewery.

1912 – Paper Mill, Little Paxton. On the 13th May at about midday, with about 200 people working there, the Paper Mill in Little Paxton near St Neots was almost completely destroyed by a fire; only the rag sorting house being left standing. The St Neots Fire Brigade were in attendance until 16.00 hours on the 15th May turning over debris and damping down. Rebuilding started immediately but this time using brick, in place of the old timber building.

1929 – St Neots. At 20.10 hours on the 27th June the Pavilion Cinema in the High Street was badly damaged by fire. St Neots firemen spent 11 hours at the scene ably assisted by crews from Sandy, Bedford, Huntingdon and Cambridge.

1930 – Eaton Socon. On Saturday evening 8th February at around 20.30 hours a small fire was discovered in the organ chamber of Eaton Socon Church. The St Neots and Sandy Fire Brigades were immediately telephoned but by the time they arrived and set their pumps into the river, some 400 yards away, and

Paper Mill fire, Little Paxton (photo – St Neots Advertiser)

then run out hoses, the church was ablaze from end to end and spreading to the 120 feet high tower. At about midnight one of the bells fell from the tower and shattered on the stone floor of the church. The church was severely damaged and the next morning the service was held on the nearby village green.

1934 – St Neots. On the 6th April the four-storey Priory Mill, alongside the river in St Neots, was badly damaged in a fire. The fire was believed to be caused by a stone or metal object entering a grinder creating a spark. An employee had a lucky escape when he was trapped by the rapidly spreading fire. He managed to escape through a ventilator onto the roof from where he was rescued by ladder. Assistance from Huntingdon Fire Brigade was requested and the flames were prevented from reaching 500 gallons of fuel oil and 1,000 sacks of grain were unaffected by the fire. A section of the mill built in 1892 was gutted but the older part built in 1782 was saved. Damage was estimated at several thousand pounds.

1935 – Wisbech. Burton's Chip Basket Factory in Oldfield Lane was destroyed by a major fire, which caused serious concerns as it was adjacent to the Shell-Mex Petrol store containing some 27,000 gallons of fuel. All of the brigade's equipment was in use and it took 16 hours to extinguish the blaze. It was estimated that 7,000 people stood to watch the fire which could be seen in Watlington 15 miles away.

PART TWO

1939–1948

Chapter 2

WARTIME & THE AFS, 1939-1941

DURING the mid 1930s it had become apparent that at some future date there would be another war with Germany. In February 1937 the first government moves to co-ordinate the fire service's readiness for war required local authorities to submit air-raid precautions and fire protection schemes for their areas. At this time there were some 1,600 fire brigades in Britain with varying levels of equipment, training and competency ranging from the large motorised city brigades down to the local village manual pump. The Air-Raid Precautions Act of 1937 made provision for grants to improve local firefighting services which included the setting up of a volunteer force to be known as the Auxiliary Fire Service (AFS) to supplement the regular fire brigades in the event of war. Later in 1938 came the Fire Brigades Act including a section, which for the first time, placed a statutory requirement on the various local authorities to maintain efficient fire brigades.

At first recruitment into the AFS was slow, but following various recruitment campaigns there was soon a steady influx of volunteers from such varied backgrounds that included solicitors, bankers, journalists, artists, salesmen, drivers and labourers. There were even a number of conscientious objectors. All emergency equipment was provided direct from the Home Office and was painted battleship grey. The vehicles included Heavy Units which were built on a number of different large commercial vehicle chassis with a self-contained pump unit mounted on a platform at the rear. The pumps had six deliveries, capable of pumping either 900 gpm or 1,400 gpm. There was also a covered shelter for the crew and equipment lockers. However, the majority of the pumps supplied were trailer pumps which sat on two-wheeled trailers suitable for towing behind light vans or family sized cars.

Personal equipment issued to the recruits consisted of a cap, overalls, rubber boots and a steel helmet. They would have to wait for some time before waterproof leggings and a fire tunic were supplied. As well as being attached to regular fire stations many small sub-stations for the AFS had been ear-marked in such places as schools, garages, factories etc. In Old Fletton, for example, a Fire Station for the AFS was built alongside the High Street premises of the Council Fire Brigade, whilst

Badge of the Auxiliary Fire Service

Example of a Bedford Heavy Unit seen here in a preserved role (photo – Gordon Townsend collection)

in Wisbech there were 12 AFS Fire Stations set up around the town, some supplied with trailer pumps whilst others had just the basic equipment of hydrant standpipes and a few lengths of hose.

When war was declared on the 3rd September 1939 the AFS was mobilised and the whole of the British Fire Services was soon on a war footing and every station was manned 24 hours a day. This caused many problems as the majority of fire stations had very basic facilities. Soon, however, huts were being built on land surrounding the stations to provide the necessary accommodation.

Most villages had not had organised fire brigades prior to the war, but with AFS units set up, now had their own firefighting force for the first time. In Swaffham Bulbeck for example, the landlord of the *Crown Inn*, Hugh Sturgess, set up the local AFS unit using the licensed premises and an 18th century barn at the rear.

When the heavy bombing raids of 1940 and 1941 were carried out on the large cities of the UK, many of the local units were called upon to support their beleaguered colleagues when mobile columns were formed, often travelling large distances.

However, it soon became apparent at these large incidents that due to the attendance of many different brigades with their different rank structures, training and equipment there was little co-ordination between them. Following complaints from many of the larger brigades, meetings were held at the Home Office in an attempt to iron out these problems and thus the idea of a National

Sages Lane, Peterborough AFS crew (photo – Gordon Townsend collection)

Old Fletton AFS crew (photo – Huntingdon County Record Office)

AFS crews and Trailer Pumps, Arbury Road, Cambridge 1940 (photo – Tony Brotchie collection)

Fire Service (NFS) was evolved and plans were soon being laid to bring all the brigades, both large and small, into one large service.

May 1941 saw a number of units from the Peterborough area attend Spalding (Lincolnshire) where the town had suffered a heavy incendiary attack.

In July 1941 Captain Horace Friend resigned as Chief Officer of the Wisbech Borough Fire Brigade after 21 years in charge. He was replaced by his son Jack, but his time as Chief Officer must have been one of the shortest in history as just a few weeks later, on the 18th August, the NFS was formed and both his rank and position were now defunct. It is interesting, however, to note that the St Neots unit of the NFS still carried on holding Brigade Meetings and in fact at the meeting in December 1941 H. Smith was still being referred to as Captain and was signing the minutes in that capacity. However, by the AGM of January 1942 the minutes noted that he now held the NFS rank of Section Leader (Sub Officer) and that the 1st and 2nd Lieutenants were holding the rank of Leading Firemen although the 'Brigade' were still electing a Secretary and Treasurer. However, a month later in February, the Brigade's Bank Account was closed and the funds shared out between the serving men.

Incidents

August 1940 – Peterborough. A damaged British Blenheim bomber, returning from a raid on enemy territory, crashed in Fengate with the loss of all of the crew.

16th January 1941 – The Perse School, Cambridge. This public school was badly damaged in an incendiary attack and a nearby garage and wireless store also suffered damage. Both the wholetime brigade and the AFS were soon on the scene but it was some hours before the fire was eventually contained. As was normal with restrictive wartime reporting the *Cambridge Daily News* could only state that a 'famous public school at an East Anglian town was badly damaged' despite the townspeople being fully aware of the situation.

16th March 1941 – Abbotsley, near St Neots. At 20.10 hours the Motor Pump from St Neots and a RAF Crash Tender attended to a RAF Hurricane fighter which had crashed near the village.

Chapter 3

THE NATIONAL FIRE SERVICE

FOLLOWING a number of high-level meetings at the Home Office, the idea of a National Fire Service (NFS) was evolved and the Fire Service (Emergency Provisions) Bill was presented to the House of Commons in May 1941. It soon went through the necessary stages and on the 22nd May received royal assent. The necessary planning and re-organisation began immediately and on the 18th August the NFS came into being. The country was divided into thirty-two Fire Force Regions, twenty-six in England and Wales and six in Scotland. Each region was further divided into divisions and companies. Cambridge was the headquarters of No. 12 Fire Force while Peterborough was within No. 9 Fire Force, with its headquarters at Leicester.

Also by this time the Home Office began issuing Auxiliary Towing Vehicles (ATV) to replace the worn out vehicles which had been in use since the formation of the AFS. These were based on the Austin K2 2-ton box van, having steel sides and a reinforced splinter-proof roof with crew seats and lift up lockers inside. Other appliances issued by the Home Office included Escape Carrying Units, which were fitted with a hosereel and towed a trailer pump. Later versions were fitted with a front mounted pump and in effect became a Pump Escape. However, the most significant appliance was the Mobile Dam Unit, which was a lorry fitted with a large water tank on the back used to ferry water to emergency dams which were set up in strategic locations. Later when fitted with a light pump, carrying hose and other firefighting equipment it became particularly useful in rural areas. It was from this rudimentary type of appliance that the modern Water Tender was born.

In Cambridge during the period 1941–45 a number of temporary stations were operational at the following sites: Arbury Road, Cheddars Lane, Coleridge Road, Downing Street, Gwydir Street, Newmarket Road, Quayside, Rathmore Road and Victoria Road. There was even a River Section operating a Fire Boat on the River Cam.

The town itself was ringed with an overground metal pipeline and numerous static water tanks. Although Cambridge itself was not severely damaged by enemy action, its firefighters, like those from many other provincial towns, assisted on numerous occasions to extinguish large fires

Badge of the National Fire Service

Example of an ATV and Trailer Pump seen here in a preserved role (photo – Gordon Townsend collection)

Example of a Fordson F7 Escape Carrying Unit – note the front mounted pump
(photo – Gordon Townsend collection)

Fireboat at Chesterton on the River Cam (photo – Tony Brotchie collection)

in such towns and cities as Coventry, Liverpool, London, Norwich, and Southampton.

In 1941 land at Dogsthorpe, in the North East of Peterborough was requisitioned and a 10 bay station, of a wooden hutted construction, was built. Other stations in use at this time were at the Baker Perkins Factory, Bishops Road, Castor, Celta Road near the Hotpoint Factory, Glinton, Halls Works in Queens Walk, High Street in Old Fletton, London Brick Co., Milton Hall, Northfield Road, Oundle Road, Perkins Diesels Factory, Queen Street (the old City Brigade Fire Station), Sages Lane in Alwalton, Werrington and the PVFB. In total there were about 400 NFS personnel serving in the city and the surrounding area.

Dogsthorpe Fire Station 1941 (photo – Author's collection)

Sawtry Fire Station 1942 seen here in the left of the picture (photo – Gordon Townsend collection)

In 1942 the NFS leased land in Ely to build a temporary war-time Fire Station to house five fire appliances. Another NFS unit to find a new home in 1942 was Sawtry, who moved to a station built in the grounds of the Manor House.

In June 1944, some three years after the NFS had been formed, a very bureaucratic message was issued to the effect that all non-service badges, e.g. AA

Old Fletton NFS crew with trailer pump (photo – Huntingdon County Record Office)

St Neots NFS crews (photo – Gordon Depledge collection)

and RAC badges carried on NFS vehicles were to be removed immediately, clearly labelled indicating which vehicle they came from and forwarded to headquarters. There is no record if any were ever returned.

By the end of the war the NFS was gearing itself down to a peacetime role and the promised return of the Fire Service to local control. However, it was not until the 1st February 1947 that the Fire Service Act was placed before Parliament. A whole era of firefighting was over and the NFS was transferred back to local authority control on the 1st April 1948, but this time there were only 147 Fire Brigades, larger than the pre-war brigades, and now the responsibility of County Councils and County Boroughs. At this time any civil brigade not maintained by such local authority, i.e. volunteer brigades, and which had managed to survive the NFS were now disbanded. The only one in the whole country which succeeded in surviving this act was the Peterborough Volunteer Brigade.

Incidents

August 1941 – Huntingdon. German bombers dropped 47 bombs on the town causing extensive damage to property.

2nd October 1941 – Wyboston. While the 46th Battalion of the Royal Tank Regiment was on manoeuvres a tank was accidentally driven into a pond at Top Farm. The driver was rescued by a crew from St Neots.

7th December 1941 – Croxton Park, Croxton. During the early part of the war the grounds of Croxton Hall were used as a petrol dump by the military and at 19.50 hours two crews from St Neots attended a fire when approximately 5,000 gallons of petrol caught alight. Foam compound and a water relay from the park's lake were used to extinguish the fire.

27th February 1942 – Wisbech. A fire in the offices of Ollard & Ollard, Solicitors, 8 York Row caused partial destruction of a building of great historical value. The fire took a swift hold due the construction of the building, which had lathed walls and a reeded roof. Destroyed in the blaze was a legal library, reputedly one of the best in the eastern counties, containing many volumes of irreplaceable value. Despite the destruction the strong room containing legal documents, ledgers, accounts etc. was saved.

9/10th August 1942 – Peterborough. It was around midnight that the worst air-raid on Peterborough occurred when around 250 incendiary bombs were dropped. Six landed on the Cathedral, others on the Bishop's Palace and a number of other buildings in the Precincts, while thirty fell on the Town Hall and the remainder fell on shops and offices in Bridge Street. Fourteen fires were started, mainly in roofs, and the situation looked alarming for a time. The greatest damage was caused to the City Cinema in Bridge Street, which was out of use for some months.

August 1942 – Ramsey. A German bomber, returning from another raid on Peterborough, discharged four high explosive bombs over Ramsey, killing seven people.

15th April 1943 – St Neots. At 17.44 hours one fire appliance was mobilised to a plane crash at Crosshall Ford followed a few minutes later when a further appliance was sent to Smiths Farm, Cambridge Street to yet another plane crash. The first incident involved an American fighter, which had crashed on open ground and was being allowed to burn out. The pilot had baled out but was killed on landing and his body removed by Army ambulance. No further information can be found regarding the second incident and although it seems highly likely that the two incidents were caused by a mid-air collision this was not reported. The last appliance returned to station at 21.55 hours.

8th May 1943 – Great Paxton. At 16.50 hours fire appliances were mobilised to a fire, following a plane crash on the Toseland Road. In total there were four pumps and a foam tender from the NFS with RAF crews also in attendance. The stop message at 23.15 hours indicated that the fire was extinguished but that two bodies had not yet been recovered, the incident being left with the RAF.

9th January 1947 – St Neots. A fire occurred at Messrs. John Raynes Smith, 49 High Street at 03.10 hours Crews from St. Neots, Huntingdon and Gamlingay attended. Damage was caused to *a double range of buildings, separated by* *a covered haulage way, of 1 and 2 floors, 250 feet by 100 feet, comprising a shop and above a flour and seasoning store, butchers factory and packing rooms. Flour and seasoning store damaged by fire, about 30 feet by 40 feet of roof off.*

2nd June 1947 – St Neots. At 23.55 hours crews were called to a serious fire at Messrs. Paine & Co. Ltd., Malt Extract Plant, Brook Street. A *make pumps 5* message was sent and pumps from Gamlingay, Papworth Everard, Huntingdon and St Ives were sent on. A Salvage Tender from Cambridge also attended. The St Neots crew finally returned to station during the late afternoon next day.

PART THREE

FIRE BRIGADES 1948 to 1965

Chapter 4

CAMBRIDGESHIRE FIRE BRIGADE

WHEN the Cambridgeshire Fire Brigade was formed in 1948 after de-nationalisation, there were ten stations in the County, two wholetime manned, both in Cambridge at Newmarket Road and St Andrew's Street, and eight retained in the villages. Mr. T. Knowles, O.B.E, Grad I Fire E. was the first Chief Fire Officer and Brigade Headquarters were set up in a house at 43 Parkside with workshops at the rear of the premises. This was to be the site on which the new Headquarters complex and fire station were built in 1965. It was also proposed that new fire stations were to be built at

Badge of the Cambridgeshire Fire Brigade

the following locations; Barrington, Comberton, Dry Drayton, Dullingham, Fulbourn and Steeple Morden, none of which have ever been built. As can be seen, the retained stations that were taken over by the brigade were very basic and had minimal facilities.

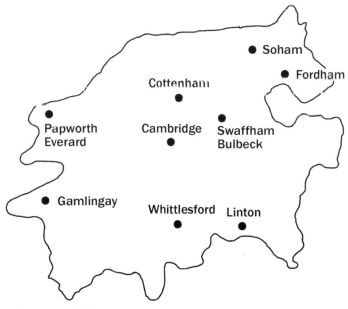

Cambridgeshire Fire Brigade, 1948

Cambridge Fire Station, Newmarket Road (photo – Tony Brotchie collection)

The appliance fleet consisted mainly of vehicles issued by the Home Office during the war and later converted to a post-war role. It is interesting to note that due to the low roofs and doors of some of the fire stations a number of the Towing Vehicles had to be adapted by fitting the extension ladder inside the appliance roof as opposed to sitting on top as per normal.

Station	Location	Appliances	Personnel
1	Newmarket Road, Cambridge	Water Tender with trailer pump Major Pump Salvage Tender with trailer pump Turntable Ladder Emergency Tender	24
2	St Andrew's Street, Cambridge	Pump Escape	10
3	High Street, Cottenham	Auxiliary Towing Vehicle with trailer pump	12
4	*Crown Inn*, Swaffham Bulbeck	Water Tender with trailer pump	5
5	Churchgate Street, Soham	Auxiliary Towing Vehicle with trailer pump	8
6	Mill Lane, Fordham	Major Pump Water Tender with trailer pump	10
7	Symonds Lane, Linton	Auxiliary Towing Vehicle with trailer pump	12
8	Duxford Road, Whittlesford	Water Tender with trailer pump	12
9	Mill Street, Gamlingay	Auxiliary Towing Vehicle with trailer pump	10
10	Papworth Industries, Papworth Everard	Water Tender with trailer pump	10

Cottenham Fire Station (photo – Tony Brotchie collection)

Fordham Fire Station (photo – Pete Ashpool)

Gamlingay Fire Station (photo – Tony Brotchie collection)

Linton Fire Station (photo – Tony Brotchie collection)

Papworth Everard Fire Station (photo – Tony Brotchie collection)

Soham Fire Station (photo – Tony Brotchie collection)

Swaffham Bulbeck Fire Station (photo – Tony Brotchie collection)

Whittlesford Fire Station (photo – Tony Brotchie collection)

The Dodge Water Tender, based at Newmarket Road, was described by retired ADO Tony Brotchie '*as being the most ill fated vehicle to have served any fire brigade*'. Apart from equipment falling off two of the crew would have to clamber along the rear of the appliance, whilst it was en-route, it order to start the pump which supplied the hosereel. This was necessary to have a ready supply of water on arrival at an incident.

At Fordham Fire Station there were difficulties in manning both appliances so it was decided to convert the 1934 Dennis Ace Limousine Pump to an Emergency Salvage Tender and it was moved to the Newmarket Road Station.

In 1950 the brigade converted an ex RAF fuel tanker into a water carrier and then in 1951 it received its first new appliance a Dennis F12 Pump Escape and by 1953 had an impressive line up of appliances, mainly of Dennis manufacture, based at the two Cambridge Fire Stations.

As mentioned in an earlier chapter the retained station at Swaffham Bulbeck had been set up with an 18th century barn as the appliance bay and the station facilities in the *Crown Inn*. The publican, Hugh Sturgess, was the Sub Officer and Tony Brotchie remembers giving lectures to the crew in the bar with bemused villagers listening in whilst supping their pints. When Hugh retired his wife, Sarah, became the unofficial caretaker and their son, Reg, took over as Sub Officer. When the *Crown Inn* closed, and was converted to a private house, one

Dodge Water Tender GXO 483 converted from a wartime vehicle (photo – Tony Brotchie collection)

Bedford QL Water Tender converted from wartime vehicle (photo – Gordon Townsend collection)

Emergency Salvage Tender converted from 1934 Dennis Ace Pump DER 640
(photo – Tony Brotchie collection)

of the downstairs rooms became the station watchroom and lecture room. Following the deaths of both Hugh and Reg Sturgess, Sarah continued in her role looking after the station and it became a tradition for any senior officer visiting the station to call in on Sarah for a chat and a cup of tea.

1950 Bedford QL Water Carrier HVE 699 converted from ex RAF fuel tanker
(photo – Tony Brotchie collection)

The period 1953–55 showed the brigade beginning to replace its retained fleet of converted water tenders with four Bedford SB limousine appliances, whilst in 1954 the first replacement station was built in Linton for the retained crew. Meanwhile in Gamlingay, the retained crew, which had been based in wooden wartime premises in Mill Street moved to a temporary station in Stocks Lane in 1955.

Cambridge line-up 1953 (l. to r.) Dennis Ace Emergency Salvage Tender DER 640, Dennis F14 Turntable Ladder LCE 212, Dennis F12 Pump Escape JVE 222, Dennis F8 Water Tender KCE 820, Dennis F8 Pump Ladder LER 999 and Dodge Water Carrier HVE 699 (photo – Tony Brotchie collection)

1953 Dennis F8 Dennis Pump Ladder LER 999 (photo – The Wardell collection)

1953 Dennis F14 Metz Turntable Ladder LCE 212 seen against the backdrop of Kings College Chapel, Cambridge (photo – Tony Brotchie collection)

1954 Bedford SB Water Tender NER 20 (photo – Tony Brotchie collection)

In April 1955 there was a change at the head of the brigade when Chief Fire Officer Knowles announced his retirement and he was replaced by Mr. R. J. Stepney, Assistant Chief Officer of Berkshire & Reading Fire Brigade. Sadly Mr Knowles was only able to enjoy a very short retirement, passing away in 1957.

Further upgrades to the appliance fleet saw the old Water Carrier replaced in 1956 by a new appliance, purpose built on the Bedford RLXZ 4×4 chassis by local body bodybuilder, Marshalls.

Further problems with manning levels at Fordham Fire Station occurred in 1957. The station had, for a number of years, never been able to muster more than seven members. Due to work commitments, the Sub Officer resigned and another two members of the crew followed suit. Despite valiant attempts the brigade was unable to locally recruit any new members and the station was closed on the 31st March. An additional appliance was stationed at Soham plus five more men recruited to cover Fordham's turnout area.

Replacement stations were opened in 1961 for the retained crews at Cottenham and Papworth Everard and by this time a further five water tenders had been purchased, this time on the Bedford RL chassis and in 1963 an Emergency Salvage Tender was purchased to replace the pre-war Dennis Ace. It was built on the Bedford RL 4×4 chassis by Papworth Industries, another local bodybuilding company. Due to the forthcoming local government boundary changes this was the final appliance purchased by the brigade.

1956 Bedford RLHZ 4×4/Marshall/Sun Water Carrier PCE 829 (photo – Pete Ashpool)

1958 Bedford RLHX 4×4/Wilsdon Water Tender VER 667 (photo – The Wardell collection)

1961 Bedford RLHX 4×4/Haydon Water Tender XVE 235 (photo – Pete Ashpool)

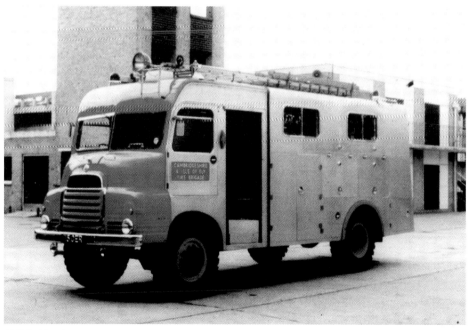

1963 Bedford RL Emergency Salvage Tender 115 CER (photo – Gordon Townsend collection)

Cambridge Fire Station – Rear view and fire house (photo – Author's collection)

Another retained crew to get a new station was Soham whose station was opened in 1964. This was a single bay station which later had an extension built onto the front to allow two appliances to be garaged in tandem, a very unusual system.

A new headquarters complex for the brigade was officially opened in February 1965, just a few weeks before the amalgamation with the Isle of Ely Fire Service, twenty-six years after the site was first acquired in 1939. The Second World War had intervened and after the war the need for housing had put the scheme in the background. In 1949 the Chief Fire Officer had put forward a report but with various objections and then a number of Treasury curbs, it was not until 1959 that approval was finally given and work eventually started in 1963. The total cost of the building and equipment was £208,000.

It is interesting to note that when the Newmarket Road Fire Station was closed and the new headquarters in Parkside opened, there was much consternation, within the city population, that the station in St Andrews Street would be closed. Although the two stations were virtually in sight of one another across Parker's Piece Green, the brigade continued to operate the Pump Escape from St Andrews Street for another year before finally closing the station.

Incidents

29th November 1949 – Pye Ltd., Madingley Road, Cambridge. One of the most serious fires during the last decade occurred when a hangar housing several thousand wireless sets, 300 to 400 television sets and numerous components were destroyed at an estimated cost of £900,000.

4th February 1951 – Abington Piggotts. A US military aircraft crashed in the early hours and burst into flames. Five members of the crew lost their lives as a result of the crash but three others managed to escape through the tail section. The fire was extinguished by the use of foam making compound and the Fire Brigade assisted in recovering the bodies.

6th November 1955 – Boxworth. The brigade was called in the early hours to a fire in a row of thatched cottages. On arrival the thatch was burning fiercely and copious quantities of water were required to extinguish the flames. There was severe damage to two cottages but the third was saved. Three pumps from Cambridge and one each from Papworth and Cottenham made up the attendance.

20th February 1956 – Laurie & McConnal, Fitroy Lane, Cambridge. On arrival of the first appliance, from Cambridge Fire Station, the fire had already gained a firm hold on a single storey structure adjoining a four-storey warehouse with the fire through the roof. Crews from thirteen fire appliances faced difficult icy and cold conditions before finally extinguishing the fire using eight jets. Damage was mainly confined to the single storey structure with slight damage to the main warehouse.

15th February 1958 – Garden House Hotel, Cambridge. Three crews from Cambridge responded to the alarm at 14.02 hours and requested a further three pumps plus the Emergency Salvage Tender. Four jets and two hosereels were used to fight the fire and by good salvage work, damage was confined to the upper floor and roof.

31st August 1959 – Department of Metallurgy, Pembroke Street, Cambridge. The brigade was called at 04.23 hours to one of the most serious fires for many years. The Pump and Turntable Ladder (Newmarket Road) and Pump Escape (St Andrews Street) responded and found a very severe fire on the top floor and through the roof. In total, eight appliances attended, two being used to relay water from the River Cam, and used nine jets to extinguish the fire. There was fire damage to the three upper floors with water damage to the ground floor and basement.

7th July 1960   Red House Farm, Hardwick. Appliances from Cambridge, Papworth, Gamlingay and Whittlesford responded following the report of an aircraft crash. On arrival it was found that a mid-air collision had occurred, between a Vampire jet with a crew of two and a Varsity aircraft with a crew of eight, killing all persons on board. A foam blanket was laid and the bodies extracted from the wreckage. RAF crash crews also attended from nearby RAF Oakington.

1st January 1961 – Radio & Television Services, Gloucester Street, Cambridge. Two pumps from Cambridge responded to the initial call at 08.31 hours and found a fire in one wing of a two-storey building with both floors and the roof alight. Additional pumps and the Turntable Ladder were requested and further appliances attended from Cambridge, Cottenham, Swaffham Bulbeck and the Chivers Works Fire Brigade. Six jets were used as well as a water relay from the River Cam using 6 inch hose laid by an AFS crew.

12th August 1961 – Radio & Television Services, Gloucester Street, Cambridge. The brigade was called again to this address at 17.40 hours and this time responded with two pumps and the Turntable Ladder. On arrival the fire had gained a good hold on a bay of the factory. A make-up message was sent and a further three pumps responded from Cambridge, Cottenham and Swaffham Bulbeck. This time five jets were used to extinguish the blaze.

13th March 1962 – Ickleton. At 06.14 hours a goods train crashed and a number of fuel tankers overturned. Fire appliances from Whittlesford and Cambridge, with additional supplies of foam compound, proceeded to the incident. A total of twelve fuel wagons were damaged and fuel was leaking from two of them onto the roadway and into ditches. The ditches were dammed to avoid pollution and the contained fuel burnt off under supervision. Crews stood by until the early evening while the tankers were righted and removed.

1963 – Rectory Farm, Great Chishill. This severe winter caused many problems, i.e. icy roads and snowdrifts. On this occasion crews had to dig their way out of a snowdrift and walk 3 miles with drifts up to their shoulders. They were called out at 20.06 hours and reached the farmhouse about 6 hours after the time of call. The crews, led by ADO Kidd, were officially commended for their devotion to duty on this occasion.

1962 Ickleton Goods Train Crash (photo – George Dunlop collection)

Fatal fire, Whaddon 1963 (photo – George Dunlop collection)

1963 Whaddon. During the severe winter of 1963 a serious fire occurred in a thatched property in the village of Whaddon. Crews from Cambridge, Gamlingay and Royston (Herts.) attended this incident. As a result of the fire one person lost their life.

10th August 1964 – Near American Cemetery, Madingley Road, Cambridge. The fire brigade was called to a serious road accident at 23.14 hours between a lorry and a private car which completely blocked the road. The three occupants of the car were released from the wreckage and taken to hospital with multiple injuries, but all subsequently died.

27th September 1964 – Cochranes Farm, Thriplow. A call was received at 12.49 hours to farm buildings alight. Two appliances from Cambridge and one from Whittleford were immediately mobilised. Strong winds and a rapidly spreading fire caused two thatched cottages on the opposite side of the road to be ignited by flying embers before the arrival of the brigade. The farmhouse and buildings covering an area approximately 200 feet by 200 feet and a large quantity of farm produce were two-thirds damaged by fire. The cottages were severely damaged but 80 per cent of the contents were salvaged by crews and neighbours. Crews were in attendance until the early evening of the following day turning over debris and damping down.

Chapter 5   **HUNTINGDONSHIRE**
                               COUNTY FIRE SERVICE

FOLLOWING the return to local authority control in 1948, the headquarters for the new County Fire Service was set up in the Market Square, Huntingdon, with one wholetime station, plus a retained complement in Princes Street, Huntingdon, the other six stations being wholly retained manned. Mr A. Easton was appointed to be the first Chief Fire Officer.

Badge of the Huntingdonshire County Fire Service

The fleet taken over from the NFS consisted of a number of pre-war pumps such as Yaxley's 1936 Leyland FT6 EW 9795, two wartime ATVs converted to Hosereel Tenders by the use of a Home Office issued conversion kit, consisting of a 100 gallon water tank, a hosereel, a power take-off and the necessary pump and pipework. Two other ATVs were converted for use as a Salvage Tender and a Hose Carrier. The remainder of the fleet consisted of wartime Water Tenders.

Station	Appliances	Personnel
1. Huntingdon	Hosereel Tender and trailer pump	13 (wholetime)
	Water Tender and trailer pump	19 (retained)
	Pump Escape	
	Hose Carrier	
	Salvage Tender	
2. Kimbolton	Water Tender and trailer pump	12 (retained)
3. St Neots	Hosereel Tender and trailer pump	19 (retained)
	Major Pump	
4. St Ives	Water Tender and trailer pump	12 (retained)
5. Ramsey	Water Tender and trailer pump	12 (retained)
	Major Pump	
6. Yaxley	Water Tender and trailer pump	15 (retained)
	Major Pump	
7. Sawtry	Water Tender and trailer pump	12 (retained)

With a two watch system in operation it is interesting to note that at Huntingdon only the Hosereel Tender was permanently manned, sometimes with only two riders. There nearly always appeared to be a man allocated to the Water Tender, supported by retained personnel, and two to the ambulance; it being a joint Fire and Ambulance Service. The remaining appliances were manned by the retained personnel.

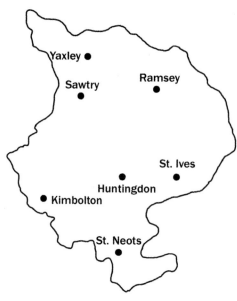

Huntingdonshire County Fire Service, 1948

During the seventeen-year life of the County Fire Service, one of the highlights of the Brigade's year was the day of the Competition Drills when teams from the various stations keenly fought to win the various trophies available for the different drills.

Huntingdon Fire Station, Princes Street (photo – Gordon Townsend collection)

Yaxley's 1936 Leyland FT6 Pump EW 9795 (photo – Gordon Townsend collection)

St Neots's 1942 Austin K2 ATV GLE 196 converted to a Hosereel Tender
(photo – Gordon Depledge Collection)

The first new fire station built by the County Fire Service opened in 1958 at Kimbolton and was built on the site of the village's very first station in Thrapston Road.

The first new post-war appliance, a Bedford Pump Escape, had been purchased in 1952 and by 1963 the last of the wartime appliances had finally been pensioned off and the fleet had been replaced by Bedford Water Tenders on the SL, TJ or TK chassis.

An additional bay was built onto the side of St Neots Fire Station side of the station in the early 1960s. In 1962 the retained unit in Ramsey moved into a new three-bay station, where a curious situation occurred during the building of the station, when the planning specification was not clearly worded. The plans showed an 'open water supply' with the intention of a covered pit being built, however, the builders quite happily complied with this by providing a small pond, which proved a hazard to both personnel and vehicles. This was, however, soon made safe by being covered over with concrete slabs. Yaxley Fire Station in the north of the county, which had been built in 1887, was extended in 1965 by adding two appliance bays onto the side of the building and converting the old appliance room into station accommodation and there were plans to rebuild all the other stations in the brigade although there were still some years to pass before all the old pre-war stations would finally disappear.

Winners of the 1954 Major Pump Drill – St Neots (left to right: Fm. Sewell, Fm. Woodward, Fm. Rapp, L/Fm. Page, Fm. Richardson, and Fm. Folbigg) (photo – Gordon Depledge collection)

Opening of Kimbolton Fire Station, 30th July 1958 (photo – Kimbolton Fire Station)

Kimbolton crew 1958 (left to right: Fm. Lilley, Fm. Fletcher, Fm. Dicks, Fm. Caress, Fm. Waite, Fm. Haynes, L/Fm. Smith, L/Fm. Sivers, and Sub O. Taylor) (photo – Kimbolton Fire Station)

1963 Bedford TJ4/Miles Water Tender 330 GEW (photo – Pete Ashpool)

St Neots Fire Station showing extension with 1963 Bedford TJ4/Miles Water Tender 337 GEW and 1952 Bedford SL/Miles Pump Escape KEW 952 (photo – Gordon Depledge collection)

1964 Bedford TKEL/HCB Angus Emergency Salvage Tender 311 CEW (photo – Tony Brotchie collection)

The final fire appliance purchased by the brigade was an Emergency Salvage Tender built on a Bedford TKEL chassis by HCB/Angus and put on the run at Huntingdon in 1964. Originally supplied painted in the standard Fire Service Red, it was later repainted white.

Incidents

27th November 1948 – Offord Cluny. At 11.00 hours a fire was reported at Offord Cluny Mill on the banks of the River Ouse. Three appliances from Huntingdon, two from St Neots and one from St Ives attended this incident. The stop message detailed '*a mill building about 100 feet by 100 feet of two, three and four floors, half well alight, part of roof off, 9 jets in use*'. Crews were at the scene until 20.00 hours.

3rd May 1951 – Brampton Crossroads. At 14.35 hours a Wellington bomber crashed into a row of houses. The Hosereel Tender and Water Tender from Huntingdon were both mobilised followed by a request for the Salvage Tender. The stop message received at 15.46 hours stated that '*all fires were out, 3 aircrew members were fatally injured and removed from the wreckage, no civilian injuries and salvage work was in progress*'.

Offord Cluny Mill 1948 (photo – *Hunts. Post*)

14th July 1951 – Huntingdon. At 17.04 hours a number of calls were received stating that a train was on fire just north of the Iron Bridge, Huntingdon. The initial attendance of the Hosereel Tender and Water Tender from Huntingdon were sent and at 17.14 hours the CFO sent a message stating that '*there were approximately 8 casualties, some serious*'. This was followed by a message '*make pumps 3*'. Fire Control ordered on Water Tenders from St Ives and Papworth (Cambridgeshire). At 19.59 hours the CFO sent the stop message '*1 passenger train, 4 coaches severely damaged by fire, 2 jets using a 3-pump relay from open water, exact number of casualties unknown*'.

20th September 1951 – Great Staughton Aerodrome. At 15.50 hours the Kimbolton crew were mobilised along with a crew from Bedfordshire to a plane crash. At 16.17 hours CFO Easton sent a stop message '*A Harvard training plane crashed, pilot received fatal injuries, 1 civilian injured attempting rescue of pilot, removed to hospital by ambulance*'. The Kimbolton crew returned to station at 18.00 hours.

15th June 1955 – St Neots. After being rebuilt following an earlier fire in 1947, Paine's Maltings in Brook Street suffered another major fire when at 01.16 hours two appliances from St Neots were mobilised. At 01.25 hours a message was sent '*make pumps 6*' which brought on three pumps from Huntingdon and one from

The burnt-out train at Huntingdon 1951 (photo – Huntingdon County Record Office)

Kimbolton. The CFO sent a further message at 02.11 hours *'make pumps 10, turntable ladders 2'*. On receipt of this message Fire Control ordered on St Ives, Gamlingay and Papworth (both Cambridgeshire) and Bedford. The Turntable Ladders were sent from Bedford and Cambridge. At 03.41 hours the stop message was sent *'Fire in three-storey mill, 85 feet by 85 feet, two-thirds well alight and roof off, 10 jets, 1 TL monitor'*. The site is now the local depot of ATS Tyres.

26th July 1955 – Eltisley. A fire at Green Farm broke out at 02.11 hours in a range of farm buildings, 120 feet by 20 feet, adjoining a stack yard. Water Tenders from St Neots and Papworth (Cambridgeshire) were sent on receipt of the initial call and at 02.45 hours a further pump and water carrier were requested. The Water Tender and Water Carrier both from Cambridge were then ordered onto the incident. Five jets from open water were used to extinguish the blaze.

Friday 13th June 1958 – Spaldwick and Wood Walton. Just after midnight Air Traffic Control at RAF Wyton advised Fire Control that they believed two aircraft had collided south of Alconbury Airfield. Two appliances from Huntingdon plus RAF and USAF Foam Tenders were mobilised. The wreckage of a RAF Canberra of 58 Squadron, from RAF Wyton, was found near the Easton Turn on the Ellington to Spaldwick Road. Meanwhile the wreckage of a T3 two-seater trainer on a flight from the USAF base at RAF Alconbury was found near to Spaldwick. The flight crews from both aircraft were all killed in the collision. About an hour later a call was received from the police advising that parts of a crashed aircraft were scattered over a wide area at Wood Walton, including the complete blockage of the main rail line to the north. In the confusion surrounding the first tragic collision a ground crew mechanic, with the 86th Squadron, 47th Bomb Wing of the USAF at Alconbury, seized his chance to takeoff in one of the squadron's B-45 Tornado Bombers. His maiden flight lasted no more than 3 minutes. The mechanic, who had no flying experience, fatally crashed the B-45 into the railway embankment at Green Arch Lane, Wood Walton.

Saturday 7th January 1961 – Melchbourne (Bedfordshire). In an example of across the border assistance, Kimbolton were mobilised at 07.34 hours to Melchbourne High Street where a row of nine thatched cottages were on fire. At 09.20 hours a message was sent to Bedfordshire Control stating that '*a row of 9 cottages with thatched roofs, 50 per cent of the roofs involved in fire, 5 jets from 4 appliances and working from hydrants*'. Kimbolton returned to station at 11.29 hours.

Saturday 12th October 1963 – Easton. A call was received at 16.18 hours to a fire at Stocking Farm. Crews from Kimbolton, Huntingdon and Thrapston (Northants.) were mobilised to find on arrival that a range of farm buildings 80 feet by 100 feet and a dutch barn containing loose straw were well alight. Six jets from open water were used to extinguish the fire. The Kimbolton crew were in attendance until just after 08.00 hours the next morning.

THE fledgling service set up in 1948 consisted of nine stations, with only Ely and Wisbech having wholetime establishments, both on a day-manning basis with retained backup and the other seven stations being fully retained manned. The first Chief Fire Officer of the service was Mr J. H. Helm. The County Council had acquired the land the war-time station at Ely was built on but despite rising maintenance costs it was not until 1970 that the building was eventually replaced.

Badge of the Isle of Ely Fire Service

The Thorney crew at this time were equipped with a pre-war Leyland Cub fire appliance, ex Wisbech, which was located in a prefabricated wartime building a few yards from the current station. Originally built as a Pump it was converted to a Water Tender by adding a 400 gallon water tank which made life more difficult for the crew by reducing the size of the rear crew cab.

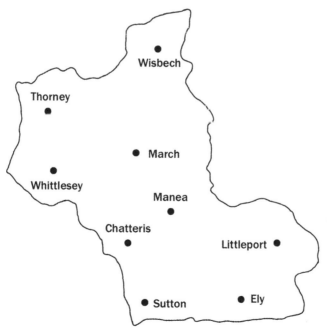

Isle of Ely Fire Service, 1948

Thorney's Leyland Cub JE 4222 (photo – Gordon Townsend collection)

In 1950 a very unusual appliance was built at Wisbech Fire Station. An ex-army Bedford QL lorry was purchased and fitted with a large rectangular water tank on the rear platform. To the front a 15 feet long arm could be attached, fitted with a claw attachment on the end. By the use of a fitted winch the arm could be used to pull apart burning hay and straw stacks.

Wartime ATV GXH 710 (ex Cambridge) (left) and 1950 Bedford QL Water Carrier conversion GYR 819 minus the stack grab (right) (photo – Ted Angus)

1961 Bedford RLHZ/Smith Water Tender NEB 945 (photo – Pete Ashpool)

1964 Bedford TKEL/HCB Pump Escape OEB 939 converted to Water Tender (photo – Pete Ashpool)

The purchase of new appliances to replace the pre-war and wartime fleet commenced in 1952–53 when three Water Tenders were supplied, built on Bedford SH chassis and then in 1956 a Water Carrier was purchased on a Bedford RL chassis. Also in 1956 a new fire station was opened in Chatteris. The purchase of Water Tenders recommenced in 1959 and by 1962 a further five had been purchased, this time on the Bedford RL chassis. The Sutton crew had a new fire station built in 1960 whilst a new station for March was opened in 1963. In 1964 two Bedford TK Pump Escapes were purchased for Ely and Wisbech, which in later years were converted to Water Tenders.

Incidents

September 1949 – Wisbech. A fire at Smedley's, Lynn Road attracted large crowds as clouds of heavy smoke swept over the town. The fire was in some 12,000 cardboard cartons each containing twenty-four empty metal cans, nearly all of which were destroyed, although the building itself was only slightly damaged.

January 1953 – Wisbech. At the time of the disastrous East Coast floods thirty-two premises in Wisbech were flooded with eleven pumps from around the local area, including Wisbech, March, Thorney and Sutton in use. Crews from over the UK were also mobilised to assist local brigades including a contingent of fifty firemen with ten pumps from Cornwall, Devon and Gloucester who were on standby at the Agricultural Ground, Friday Bridge.

February 1954 – Wisbech. Flames swept through the premises of Messrs. Foster & Sons, Chapel Road. The 100-year-old building contained a hardware shop, carpenters shop, saw mill and a box making shop. Only a change of wind saved the Corn Exchange and the *Wisbech Arms* public house from being involved in the blaze. Most of the building and contents were destroyed.

Chapter 7

SOKE OF PETERBOROUGH FIRE BRIGADE

THE 'Soke' was an area traditionally associated with the city of Peterborough. When county councils were created for the first time in 1888, in recognition of its special status, it became an independent administrative county.

Badge of Soke of Peterborough Fire Brigade

The first Chief Fire Officer of the brigade was thirty-nine year old Walter 'Bill' Bunday who had joined the Fire Service in the 1930s in his native London. Prior to his appointment there had been two wholetime stations in Peterborough; Oundle Road and Dogsthorpe. The original intentions were to base the new brigade at Oundle Road but CFO Bunday showed a preference for Dogsthorpe and the Fire Brigade Committee backed him and the rest is history. Oundle Road was closed and Dogsthorpe Fire Station, as it has always been known, became the headquarters of the Soke of Peterborough Fire Brigade. The wholetime station was backed up by the Peterborough Volunteer Fire Brigade at King Street Fire Station. Also at this time the station at Old Fletton was closed as the area could be covered by the Peterborough stations. The wholetime staff of the brigade consisted of the CFO and his deputy, one Station Officer, two Sub Officers, four Leading Firemen and twenty-four firemen. The disposition of appliances and their manning was as follows:

Dogsthorpe Fire Station
Pump Escape and Turntable Ladder (permanent manning).
Pump (Heavy Unit) and Water Tender with trailer pump (alternate manning).

PVFB (King Street)
Major Pump and ATV with trailer pump (volunteer manning).

In 1950 the brigade received its first post-war appliance; a Dennis F12 Pump Escape and this was followed in 1956 by another appliance, this time a Water Tender on the Dennis F8 chassis. In 1957 an unusual appliance was purchased by Peterborough, a Thorneycroft Nubian Water Tender. Nubian appliances normally being used for airfield crash tenders. A return to the Dennis marque was made in 1962 when a F24 Pump Escape was purchased.

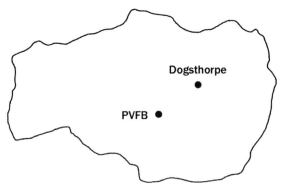

Soke of Peterborough Fire Brigade, 1948

'Out with the old and with the new' – 1944 Dodge Water Tender GXO 483 (ex NFS) and 1957
Thorneycroft Nubian Water Tender GFL 507 (photo – Gordon Townsend collection)

By the early 1960s the service had outgrown the wartime station at
Dogsthorpe and a modern headquarters with a five-bay station was built on the
same site and officially opened in 1964.

The final appliances purchased by the brigade were in 1965 and consisted of a
Bedford TKEL Emergency Salvage Tender with bodywork by Dennis Brothers,
which replaced a trailer unit towed by the Water Tender. This appliance was
originally painted red, but later modified and repainted white. Also that year a
Turntable Ladder built on an AEC Mercury chassis with a 100-foot Merryweather ladder was purchased to replace the 1943 Dennis Lancet appliance.

Incidents

15th February 1951 – Oundle Road, Peterborough. At 20.11 hours a call
was received to a fire at the premises of Midland Tar Distillers. Two pumps were

1957 line-up at Dogsthorpe; left to right Thorneycroft Nubian WrT GFL 507, Dennis F12 PE AEG 303, Dennis TL GLW 436, Fordson Heavy Unit (photo Gordon Townsend collection)

mobilised from Dogsthorpe and the PVFB. CFO Bunday also attended and on arrival he sent a message '*make pumps 4, foam compound required*'. Additional pumps were sent from Yaxley (Hunts.), Stamford and Crowland (both Lincs.) and Thrapston (Northants.). Sixty-four gallons of foam compound was sent up the A1 from Huntingdon. The stop message at 22.04 hours was '*fire in building of ½ acre containing 7 storage tanks and pitch bed, approximately half severely damaged by fire*'.

30th July 1954 – The Maltings, Midland Road, Peterborough. At 05.23 hours the Pump Escape and Turntable Ladder from Dogsthorpe and one pump from the PVFB were despatched to this address where a fire was reported in a building of two and three floors and a semi-basement. On arrival, the upper floor and roof were well alight and a message '*make pumps 5*' was sent. The additional appliances came from Yaxley (Hunts.), Oundle (Northants.), Stamford and Bourne (both Lincs.). Two jets and the Turntable Ladder monitor were used to extinguish the fire and the stop message was sent at 06.34 hours. The fire brigade was in attendance until 10.25 hours on the 2nd August.

1955 – Near Peterborough Station. The 15.50 hours train from Kings Cross to Leeds had just left Peterborough Station and was passing under Westwood Bridge when the locomotive and the first two coaches derailed and overturned. Luckily there were only a few injuries due to the slow speed of the train, but four passengers were taken to hospital. The accident happened just after employees of the local Baker Perkins factory had 'clocked off' work and the throng of people soon blocked the bridge. Equipment had to be manhandled, through the crowds, to the scene.

22nd August 1956 – Cowgate, Peterborough. The Robert Sayles department store was locked up for the night at 18.20 hours but at about 18.45 hours a passer-by, seeing flames within the store alerted the nearby police post in the old Town Hall. The police informed fire control at Dogsthorpe at 18.50 hours. Dogsthorpe Fire Station turned out with a Pump Escape and Turntable Ladder and the call bells for the PVFB were activated. Meanwhile a policeman grabbed a brick and broke a glass door to gain entry. The inrush of air caused a flashover and the fire spread rapidly. Members of the PVFB responding from their nearby shops and homes found that their station was at risk of being engulfed in the fire and sent an immediate message '*make pumps 5*'. Eventually twelve appliances from the two Peterborough Fire Stations, Sawtry and Yaxley (Hunts.), Thorney and Whittlesey (Isle of Ely), Oundle (Northants.), Stamford (Lincs.) and three local works brigades attended along with two huge American pumps from USAF Alconbury, neither of which could be used due to the incompatibility of their equipment. At 20.30 hours an informative message was sent as follows '*a range of buildings of three and four floors well alight, at work with 11 jets, fire under control*' to be followed at 21.02 hours with the message '*stop for Cowgate, knocking off some jets but appliances will be detained for some time*'. Crews were in attendance

Robert Sayle's store fire 1956, Dogsthorpe's TL at work (photo – Gordon Townsend collection)

Robert Sayle's store fire 1956 (photo – Peterborough Volunteer Fire Brigade)

'The day after' – aftermath of the Robert Sayle's store fire (photo – Peterborough Volunteer Fire Brigade)

until the evening of the following day. The construction of the store; timber floors, matchboard lining, open lift shaft and staircase, large areas of glazing, which collapsed and vented the fire, all allowed rapid spread of fire. The highly combustible contents of loosely stacked materials and furnishings also helped. The insurable loss was set at £250,000; quite a considerable figure at that time.

April 1960 – Peterborough United Football Club, Peterborough. A fire broke out in the Directors' Room and Bar in the main grandstand. Part of the bar and much of the roof was damaged before it was brought under control. If the fire had not been detected so quickly then the grandstand itself might well have been totally destroyed, due to its wooden structure.

PART FOUR

FIRE BRIGADES 1965 to 1974

Chapter 8

CAMBRIDGESHIRE & ISLE OF ELY FIRE BRIGADE

FOLLOWING the re-organisation of local government in 1965 the Cambridgeshire Fire Brigade and Isle of Ely Fire Service were amalgamated into one Brigade; appropriately named the Cambridgeshire & Isle of Ely Fire Brigade, with the headquarters and control room based at Cambridge Fire Station. The brigade was divided into two divisions; North Division with its headquarters at Wisbech and South Division based at Cambridge with the Chief Fire Officer of Cambridgeshire Mr. R. J. Stepney taking over the post for the new combined brigade.

Badge of the Cambridgeshire & Isle of Ely Fire Brigade

Cambridge Control Room (photo – Tony Brotchie collection)

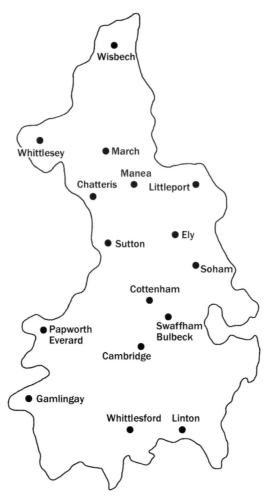

Cambridgeshire & Isle of Ely Fire Brigade, 1964

One of the first actions for the new brigade was to open a new fire station at Littleport in 1965. A similar station was opened in Gamlingay in 1966 on the site of the temporary station in Stocks Lane. Whilst building work was being carried out the Gamlingay appliance was kept in the premises of a local car dealership. In 1966 the brigade purchased two Bedford RLHZ Water Tenders and an Emergency Tender was supplied to Wisbech built on a long wheel base Land Rover.

At Whittlesey a new fire station was opened in 1967, unusual for a retained crew in that it was a two storey building. Another new appliance for Wisbech was a Water Carrier built in 1968 by HCB Angus also on the Bedford RLHZ chassis.

From 1969 to 1974 a further eight Water Tenders on the Bedford TKEL chassis were purchased, all built by HCB Angus. In 1970, after a wait of many

1966 Bedford RLHZ/HCB Angus Water Tender EJE 137D (photo – Pete Ashpool)

1967 Land Rover Emergency Tender GCE 481E (photo – Gordon Townsend collection)

1968 Bedford RLHZ/HCB Angus Water Carrier HVE 939F (photo – Pete Ashpool)

1972 Bedford TKEL/HCB Angus Water Tender Ladder WCE 682L (photo Pete Ashpool)

1972 ERF/Simon SS50 Pump Hydraulic Platform SVE 668K (photo – Gordon Townsend collection)

years, Ely had a new Fire Station built on the site of the old war time station, in Egremont Street. The work had been phased in order that fire cover could be maintained without a break.

The Chief Fire Officer, R. J. Stepney, announced his resignation in 1970 to take up a position in industry and on the 1st September the Deputy Chief Officer, Mr. Cecil Carey, was promoted to take his place.

Since the late 1960s the fire station at Whittlesford had been rapidly becoming obsolete with no room on the site for expansion. Investigations found

1973 Bedford KG 4×4/Gladwins Water Carrier WJE 265L (photo – Pete Ashpool)

Fire in *Turks Head* public house, Trinity Street, Cambridge, 1967 (photo – Tony Brotchie collection)

that no alternative site in the village was available, but with industry growing in nearby Sawston, a further search was made there and subsequently a new station was built and opened in 1971 and the Whittleford unit was closed.

In 1972 the brigade purchased a new type of appliance, an ERF Pump Hydraulic Platform to replace the 1951 Dennis Pump Escape. Another Water Carrier was purchased, in 1973, this time for Cambridge on a Bedford TKM 4×4 chassis and built by Gladwins, a local bodybuilder.

Incidents

17th April 1967 – Brook End, Steeple Morden. Crews from Cambridge, Gamlingay and Royston (Herts.) were mobilised at 16.19 hours when a Canberra aircraft crashed and hit a farmhouse. On arrival a make-up message was sent '*make pumps 5*'. The second pump from Royston and one from Potton (Beds.) were then despatched to the incident. Crash Tenders from RAF Bassingbourn were also in attendance and two water jets and RAF foam monitors were used to extinguish the flames. The bodies of the three crew members were recovered from the wreckage and fortunately there were no civilian fatalities.

18th December 1967 – *Turks Head Grill*, Trinity Street, Cambridge. A fire, which had been burning for several hours in the top floor, was not discovered until it burst through the roof at 04.00 hours. Three appliances from Cambridge were despatched on receipt of the call and on arrival sent a message '*make pump 5, turntable ladder required*'. The construction of the building, the proximity of other buildings and the limited access posed problems for the crews who used four jets and the turntable monitor to put out the blaze. The top floor and roof were severely damaged but excellent salvage work (thirty salvage sheets were used) helped to minimize further damage to the rest of the building. Trinity Street itself was closed for several hours.

September 1969 – Whittlesford. A fire in a row of thatched cottages caused severe damage to the properties. Crews from Cambridge, Whittlesford and Linton dealt with this blaze.

31st December 1969 – Metal Box Ltd., Weasenham Lane, Wisbech. On New Years Eve a disastrous fire occurred in a warehouse 300 feet × 100 feet containing ten assembly lines for the manufacture of food cans and a finished stock of 3 million cans. Crews from Wisbech were soon in attendance and quickly requested additional pumps. Seventy firemen used twelve jets to save the assembly lines, although the warehouse was badly damaged and the entire stock of cans was destroyed. Appliances in attendance were from Wisbech (2) plus Water Carrier and Emergency Tender, March (2), Manea, Whittlesey, Ely and Chatteris. Huntingdonshire & Peterborough appliances in attendance were

Crews seen at work at thatched cottage fire, Whittleford 1969 (photo – Tony Brotchie collection)

The Metal Box Company Warehouse Fire, 1969 (The George Dunlop collection)

from Dogsthorpe, PVFB and Thorney whilst West Walton, Outwell and Terrington St Clement attended from Norfolk. Long Sutton in Lincolnshire completed the attendance.

19th February 1972 – Regent Wharf, Wisbech. The Motor Vessel *Tillerman*, fully loaded with spirit and gas oil, went aground across the River Nene on the outgoing tide. There were fears that the ship might break her back and arrangements were made to pump the spirit and oil ashore to reduce the dead weight. A serious fire was a possible consequence if the ship should break up and extensive arrangements were made for the standby of fire appliances and foam. Four fire appliances from Wisbech and March were in attendance at the incident and four others from March, Manea, West Walton and Outwell, the last two from Norfolk were stationed at Wisbech Fire Station to respond to other incidents and to be available as reinforcements to the incident if required. Fortunately the vessel was safely refloated after 12 hours without damage or fire.

24th April 1972 – Garden House Hotel, Cambridge. One of the most serious fires experienced by the Brigade occurred on this Monday morning. There were thirty-five guests and eleven staff occupying the premises when at approximately 05.30 hours several guests were awakened by smoke entering their rooms. The corridors were heavily smoke-logged and the occupants escaped via the windows, with the exception of two elderly female guests, whose bodies were later recovered by firemen. The fire had reached serious proportions before discovery and to such an extent that the telephone could not be used to make an emergency 999 call. A call was eventually received at Control at 05.53 hours and the first attendance of three appliances from Cambridge were

Garden House Hotel – note the portable pumps set into the River Cam (photo – *Cambridge Evening*

mobilised immediately and on arrival found the reception area was well alight with guests escaping on to the flat roofs at first floor level. Reinforcements were requested by radio and in total ten pumps, the Turntable Ladder and Pump Hydraulic Platform attended the fire.

3rd August 1972 – Sydney Sussex College, Cambridge. More than 100 shoppers and tourists gathered to watch a fire in student accommodation above shops in Sussex Street. The fire was first spotted by shoppers who saw flames

ERF Pump Hydraulic Platform at work Sussex Street, Cambridge, 1972
(photo – Tony Brotchie collection)

coming through a first floor bedroom window. Cambridge Fire Station attended with two pumps, Pump Hydraulic Platform and Turntable Ladder and the fire was confined to the room of origin.

28th November 1972 – Cheffin, Grain & Chalk, Cambridge. Seven fire appliances from Cambridge, Swaffham Bulbeck, Sawston and Cottenham attended a serious fire at 03.25 hours at this Estate Agents office in Regent Street. The fire was extinguished by the use of six jets and six BA were used. Severe damage was caused to 60 per cent of the building and contents and the fire also spread to an adjoining shop and store.

Chapter 9

HUNTINGDONSHIRE & PETERBOROUGH COUNTY FIRE SERVICE

WHEN local government was re-organised in this area, Huntingdonshire and the Soke of Peterborough were joined together to form one local authority and the Huntingdonshire and Peterborough County Fire Service came into being. Also at the same time Thorney Fire Station was moved across the border from the Isle of Ely into the new authority.

The headquarters for the new brigade was based at Dogsthorpe, Peterborough with two divisions – North based at Dogsthorpe and South based in

Badge of the Huntingdonshire & Peterborough County Fire Service

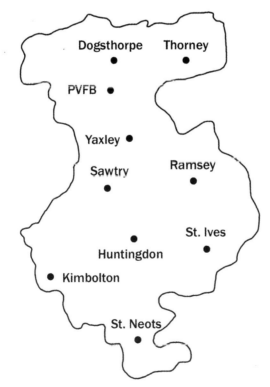

Huntingdonshire & Peterborough County Fire Service, 1974

The Service's Control Room at Headquarters (photo – Author's collection)

Huntingdon. The first Chief Fire Officer of the new brigade was Walter 'Bill' Bunday M.B.E., the former Chief Officer of the Soke of Peterborough Fire Brigade. He retired in February 1969 and was replaced by John Maxwell O.B.E., D.F.C. (Bar), Q.F.S.M.

The newly amalgamated service purchased three new appliances in its first year. A Water Tender Ladder on a Bedford TJ4 chassis, bodied by Dennis Miles,

1966 Bedford RLHZ/HCB Angus Water Tender FEW 883D, seen here in 1972 in the old NFS Thorney Fire Station (photo – Gordon Townsend collection)

was stationed at Huntingdon and two Water Carriers were purchased on the Bedford RL chassis for Huntingdon and Dogsthorpe. During the time of the Huntingdon and Peterborough County Fire Service, a total of fifteen Bedford Water Tenders were purchased; some on the RL and TJ chassis but pre-

1970 ERF Firefighter Water Tender MEW 385H (photo – Gordon Depledge collection)

1973 Bedford TKEL/HCB Angus Water Tender HEG 700L (photo – Pete Ashpool)

dominantly of the TK type. However, as a break from Bedford appliances, during the period 1969–74 three ERF fire appliances were purchased.

During the time of the Huntingdonshire and Peterborough County Fire Service half of the fire stations were replaced with new buildings. Following the Second World War a retained unit had been formed at Sawtry and it moved into a new fire station in October 1966, the third different station in the village. In August 1967 a new Divisional Headquarters and Fire Station for the South Division was opened in Hartford Road, Huntingdon and then in 1968 St Neots moved a few hundred yards along Huntingdon Street from the old station to a new three-bay station, which was eventually upgraded to day-manning status in 1973. A new two-bay station was built at St Ives and opened in 1971 and this has since been extended to include premises for the Occupational Health Department and accommodation for personnel attending courses at the Training Centre in nearby Huntingdon. The last of the new stations was opened in 1972 for the Thorney crew.

In 1972 a serving fireman from Huntingdon Fire Station, Vic Howell, was elected Mayor of the town. During his inaugural ceremony his colleagues from the station honoured him by acting as the Mayor's Escort, complete with brass helmets.

Inauguration of Fm. Vic Howell as Mayor of Huntingdon (photo – Gordon Townsend Collection)

Ramsey Fire Station crew (photo – Author's collection)

Unusual for the time, the retained stations at Kimbolton and Ramsey had retained firewomen carrying out watchroom duties. They were part of the station complement and would respond whenever there was a call-out for their crews and stay on duty until the men returned to station

Incidents

Mid- to late-1960s – A1. Before the A1 Trunk Road was made into a dual carriageway there were many serious and fatal accidents on the stretch between Eaton Socon and Southoe, known locally as 'suicide mile'. Two examples of the incidents dealt with by fire crews on this stretch of road are shown on the next page.

Sunday, 5th March 1967 – Conington. Just before midnight, the overnight mail express from Kings Cross to Edinburgh, travelling at over 80 mph on a straight stretch of line, with 200 passengers on board the eleven-coach train had just passed a signal box near Conington about 1 mile to the east of the A1 trunk road, when it was derailed. The major accident procedure was invoked, which involved the despatch of four Water Tenders, two Emergency Tenders and six ambulances. All off duty officers were informed and CFO Bunday went on to the incident. On arrival crews found a scene of horrific devastation with

RTA between two heavy goods vehicles on the A1 at Eaton Socon (photo – Gordon Depledge collection)

RTA between two private cars with both drivers killed instantly on the A1 at Crosshall
(photo – Gordon Depledge collection)

four carriages laying on their sides, the remainder of the train having come to a halt some half a mile up the line. Lighting was rigged from the Emergency Tenders and coaches were systematically searched and casualties and uninjured passengers assisted from the wreckage. A number of casualties, who had obviously been thrown from the carriage windows, were trapped between the sides of the overturned coaches and the ground and these were released by means of the 50 ton hydraulic jacks carried on the Emergency Tenders. The Chief Officer despatched the stop message at 00.30 hours and in total five persons died in the accident and a further eighteen were taken to hospital suffering from a variety of injuries.

Monday, 4th September 1967 – Great Gransden. At 14.25 hours Control Staff were alerted to fire in a thatched property in Fox Street. The first informative message at 14.48 hours advised that '*a thatched cottage was well alight and that the fire had spread to the roof of an opposite cottage*'. This was described as probably the worst house fire in the area for more than 2 years and was believed to have been caused by a spark from a bonfire setting fire to the roof of an empty cottage, which was virtually destroyed with only parts of walls and a chimney left standing. The fire spread to a 400-year-old house just across the narrow street, burning off the roof, parts of which crashed down onto bedroom floors which

The damaged thatched cottages in Fox Street, Great Gransden (photo – Gordon Depledge collection)

then caved in. Two crews from St Neots were assisted by Gamlingay and Papworth crews from Cambs. & Isle of Ely Fire Brigade. The stop message at 15.03 hours stated '*a 2-storey thatched building, approximately 33 feet by 25 feet, well alight and a 2 storey thatched building, 50 feet by 30 feet, two thirds of roof and first floor alight, at work with 5 jets from water tenders, hydrants and open water*'.

Sunday, 3rd December 1967 – St Ives. In the early hours of this Sunday morning a serious fire broke out at Kiddles Furniture Warehouse on the corner of Bridge Street and High Street. The flames threatened to jump a 6 feet gap between the warehouse and adjacent shops and a number of residents were evacuated from nearby flats. The warehouse was gutted and stock was destroyed to the value of £8,000. The fire was contained to the warehouse, although a flat and its contents in one end of the building were destroyed. Six appliances from St Ives, Huntingdon and Ramsey were in attendance and at 05.22 hours the Chief Fire Officer sent the following stop message, '*Fire in building of 3 storeys, 50 feet by 80 feet, fire in 3rd floor and roof, 6 jets in use*'.

Monday, 11th March 1968 – Peterborough. Two goods trains collided at Fletton, a few yards south of the Peacock Bridge. Two men died in the cab of one of the locomotives and a third railman was trapped for ten hours by a fractured leg whilst firemen fought to free his foot. It happened when their goods train ploughed into the back of a stationary freight train. Metal trucks at the rear of the freight train jack-knifed and crushed the cab. Following the crash the Chief Fire Officer commented on the inadequacy of the equipment carried on the appliances, particularly when dealing with heavy gauge metals. As a consequence the Cengar Saw, powered by compressed air, became standard equipment on the County's front line appliances.

Saturday, 25th May 1968 – St Neots. Just after midnight both appliances from St Neots were mobilised to Pulman Pulverisers, a plastics factory in the old granary, Station Road. The attendance of further appliances was requested and pumps from Huntingdon (2) and Kimbolton were quickly on the scene. Pumps from Gamlingay and Papworth, both from Cambridgeshire & Isle of Ely Fire Brigade, were also sent as well as a Turntable Ladder from Bedford. The stop message sent by the Chief Fire Officer at 02.13 hours read as follows, '*a building of 4 floors, approximately 100 feet by 40 feet of traditional construction, a large quantity of plastic materials in factory yard and 6 railway wagons severely burned by fire, 6 jets in use*'. Over the next few days there were a number of further calls to this incident when fires broke out in the debris remaining from the original fire.

Tuesday, 28th May 1968 – Peterborough. Peterborough suffered its biggest fire for 12 years when Brierleys, a large store in Bridge Street, was completely gutted with a loss of stock valued at £115,000. The fire brigade was alerted by AFA just before 01.00 hours and on arrival crews from the two Peterborough stations, including the Turntable Ladder, supported by the crew from

Pulman Pulverisers, St Neots – clearing up the next day (photo – Gordon Depledge collection)

Yaxley found the building already a blazing inferno. The fire was under control within an hour but the greater part of the store had been destroyed. Ironically extensions to the building were being planned and a sprinkler system was to be installed, parts for which were already on site. If the fire had occurred after the system had been fitted it would probably have controlled the blaze.

12th February 1969 – Peterborough. Soon after 01:00 hours the fire brigade were called to a fire at the Hotpoint factory. The fire broke out in a basement below a refrigeration plant. Eight appliances including the Turntable Ladder rushed to the blaze and found on arrival that the basement was heavily smoke logged. Four BA wearers with two jets entered, but searching for the fire itself was made difficult due to the large quantities of stacked combustibles and it soon became apparent that attempts to contain the fire were impossible and the crews were withdrawn just in time. Flames spread rapidly throughout the basement store area and up through conveyor belt openings to the floor above, with walls and floors cracking in the severe heat. A nearby wing contained large quantities of isocyanates, a very dangerous chemical, as well as expensive machinery and paint spray booths. Stopper jets and the turntable monitor were positioned in an attempt to stop this spread, which proved successful and after three hours the fire was under control and stopped before reaching the dangerous chemicals.

Sunday, 6th July 1969 – A1 Eaton Socon. In the days before the A1 Great North Road was made into a dual carriageway and bypassed Eaton Socon, there

The interior of the damaged coach (photo – Gordon Depledge collection)

were many road traffic accidents on the stretch between the Black Cat and Buckden, but none more horrifying than the one which occurred just after a peaceful Sunday lunchtime. The accident which occurred on Dirt House Hill, near to where the Kimbolton Road now crosses the A1, was caused when an articulated low loader was carrying a large earthmover, the blade of which ripped out the side of a coach travelling in the opposite direction. A car was also involved in the accident and sadly four passengers on the coach received fatal injuries and many others were taken to hospital with serious injuries. Local fire crews were involved in releasing trapped casualties and assisted ambulance crews with first aid to the injured.

PART FIVE

1974 to date

Chapter 10

YET another re-organisation took place on the 1st April 1974 when the number of Fire Authorities was reduced across the whole of Great Britain. This caused the amalgamation of the Cambridgeshire & Isle of Ely Fire Brigade and the Huntingdonshire & Peterborough County Fire Service into one large unit. In an innovative move, the new Chief Fire Officer John Maxwell, O.B.E., D.F.C. (Bar), Q.F.S.M., named it the Cambridgeshire Fire & Rescue Service and created the first British Fire Authority to include the word 'Rescue' in its title.

Badge of the Cambridgeshire Fire & Rescue Service

The new Fire Authority obtained the use of Hinchingbrooke Cottage, located in the grounds of Hinchingbrooke Park, Huntingdon for its new headquarters. However, until the building had been converted, a temporary headquarters was opened at Cambridge Fire Station.

Operationally the new service was divided into two divisions; North Division based at Dogsthorpe and South Division based at Cambridge and initially the Fire & Rescue Service ran with two separate Fire Controls, one in each division. When the Headquarters departments moved from Cambridge, the two controls remained in their separate locations until 1986 when an extension was built at Hinchingbrooke Cottage to house a new control suite combining the two controls.

The Divisions were further sub-divided into six Districts based at Cambridge, Ely, Huntingdon, Peterborough (Dogsthorpe), St Neots and Wisbech each with an Assistant Divisional Officer in charge and having a number of satellite stations under him. However, in the early 1980s these Districts were removed and the officers moved to the Divisional Headquarters.

With the expansion of Peterborough and its 'New Town' status, three additional fire stations were planned to provide a better service to the city. Stanground Fire Station was opened in 1977 in the south of the city but the proposed plans for stations in the Bretton and Castor areas have never been progressed.

During the period 1974–78 the service purchased nineteen Dodge Water Tender Ladders, the first six on the K850 chassis with bodywork by HCB Angus

Cambridgeshire Fire and Rescue Service 1974

Fire & Rescue Service Headquarters, Hinchingbrooke Cottage (photo – Author's collection)

1975 Dodge K850/HCB Angus Water Tender PVE 832N (photo – Mike Sudds)

and the remainder on the K1113 chassis; five bodied by HCB Angus, four by ERF and four by CFE.

In May 1978 the Cambridgeshire Fire & Rescue Service handed over to the Fire Services Museum Trust a 1953 Bedford S type Water Tender which had spent the majority of its working life at Gamlingay Fire Station. The keys were

1977 Dodge K1113/ERF Firefighter Water Tender NVE 198R (photo – Pete Ashpool)

Handing over ceremony of LVE 562 – left to right: ADO H. Wilby (Transport Officer), CFO J. C. Maxwell, Councillor J. Mitham, CFO R. Haley, Sub O. R. Hughes (OIC Gamlingay), DCFO J. Spence and M. Cole (photo – The Fire Brigade Society Library)

handed over to the Chairman of the Trust, CFO R. Haley (Bedfordshire) by Councillor J. Mitham, Chairman of the Public Protection Committee.

Since the Second World War the appliance at Manea had been stationed in a converted barn at Bearts Farm. This was always intended to be a temporary station but it was not until 1978 that the crew at Manea eventually moved into modern premises in Westfield Road.

In 1979 the Works Fire Brigade at Tillotsons Ltd. in Burwell was taken over by The Fire & Rescue Service as a retained unit and has served the county ever since.

1979 saw the purchase of two Water Tender Ladders on the Dodge G1313 chassis with bodywork by HCB/Angus. A similar appliance was supplied the following year. 1979 also saw the first 'special' appliance purchased; a Turntable Ladder for Cambridge Fire Station on a Shelvoke & Drewry chassis with a Metz 100 ft ladder and bodywork by Bensons.

Two new Rescue Tenders were built in 1980; one each for Cambridge and Dogsthorpe on Stonefield P6000 6×4 chassis and between 1980 and 1982 four Bedford TKG Water Tender Ladders were purchased, bodied by HCB Angus.

In 1981 an extension was built onto Ely Fire Station to house a museum containing old fire appliances and associated equipment and 1982 saw the supply of three strange looking fire appliances when the bodybuilders CMC of Market

The old fire station, Bearts Farm, Manea (photo – Gordon Townsend collection)

1979 Shelvoke & Drewry/Metz/Benson Turntable Ladder WVE 742T (photo – Gordon Townsend collection)

Deeping (Lincs.) supplied two Water Tender Ladders and a Rescue Vehicle/ Control Unit. Known locally as 'Rubik Cubes' the appliances were unusual in that there were no curves in the bodywork only straight edges.

1983 saw the beginning of a long relationship between the Fire & Rescue Service and Dennis fire appliances. A total of forty-six Water Tender Ladders on

1980 Dodge G1313/HCB Angus Water Tender Ladder BJE 360V (photo – Author's collection)

1980 Stonefield P6000 6×4/CMC Rescue Tender DEB 896V (photo – Pete Ashpool)

1980 Bedford TKG/HCB Angus Water Tender BVA 16V (photo – Author's collection)

1982 Bedford TKG/CMC Water Tender Ladder SEG 800X (photo – Author's collection)

the various RS chassis were purchased in the period up to 1995. All were bodied by John Dennis Coachbuilders (JDC) with the exception of just five by Fulton & Wylie in 1988.

The Cambridgeshire Fire & Rescue Service has always been at the forefront of the British Fire Service with many original ideas later taken up by other services. One of these was the change in the 1980s to the use of Aqueous Film

1982 Bedford TKG/CMC Rescue Tender/Control Unit SEG 802X (photo – Author's collection)

1988 Dennis RS135/Fulton & Wylie Water Tender Ladder E742 KEG (photo – David Palmer)

Forming Foam (AFFF) on its front line fire appliances. Prior to this change, special foam making equipment and foam compound, carried in 5-gallon cans, had to be used to supply firefighting foam. It is necessary to use foam to extinguish fires involving petrol and other liquid fires by forming a blanket across the top of burning liquid. By an ingenious design, a tank of AFFF was fitted into fire appliances and when required this was pressurised by air from the vehicle breaking system. The foam was then fed into the pump of the fire appliances by internal pipework and from there direct into the hosereels or main jet as required. All this was carried out by the pump operator operating two valves, in a matter of a few moments, to give the correct ratio of AFFF and water.

Another innovation from Cambridgeshire, in the mid 1980s, was the design of a 'fail safe' system to deal with radiation risks. Following consultation with the brigade's scientific advisor on radiation and hazardous substances, a scheme similar to the Emergency Action Code (Hazchem) used on vehicles carrying hazardous loads was designed.

Information on locations of all radioactive substances is received from the Department of the Environment by the brigade and transposed into a three-section code. These details are included on the premise risk record and also the relevant Hazrad code is labelled at the risk.

The information is decoded on the fireground with the aid of a pocket guide, which is issued to all personnel and appliances. The scheme has proved successful and has been taken up by fire brigades as far away as Australia.

The 1979 Shelvoke & Drewry Turntable Ladder had been badly damaged when it rolled over en-route to a 'shout' and in 1984 two new Turntable

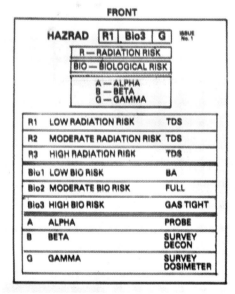

The Cambridgeshire Hazrad pocket guide (Cambridgeshire Fire & Rescue Service)

| R2 | Bio3 | G |

A typical Hazrad code (Cambridgeshire Fire & Rescue Service)

1984 Iveco 192D14/Carmichael/ Magirus Turntable Ladder A621 SEW (photo – Author's collection)

Ladders were purchased, for Cambridge and Dogsthorpe, on the Iveco 192D13 chassis, with bodywork by Carmichael and fitted with Magirus 100 ft ladders.

A GMC C20NC Rescue Tender was purchased in 1984 and based at Cambridge. The following year, 1985, saw Carmichaels build a Water Carrier on a Bedford TKM 4×4 chassis for Wisbech. A similar appliance was supplied to Cambridge in 1987.

1986 saw the introduction of the first appliance specifically 'on the run' to deal with chemical and other hazardous incidents. A Ford Transit Chemical Incident Unit towing a trailer was put on the run at St Neots to deal with the ever increasing number of calls involving dangerous substances. Not only did it carry equipment to contain and neutralise spillages, it was designed to remove contaminates in a safe and secure manner.

In the late 1980s plans were submitted to redevelop the Town Centre in Wisbech. These plans included building a supermarket on the site of the fire station in Horsefair and building a new station away from the Town Centre. The plans were approved and the new station in Churchill Road was opened in 1987.

For her unselfish service to the village fire station Sarah Sturgess, the caretaker at Swaffham Bulbeck was awarded the British Empire Medal in 1988 and later, following her death, she was given a service guard of honour at her funeral and her coffin was carried by members of the Swaffham Bulbeck crew.

1984 GMC C20NC/Woodway Rescue Tender B216 NVT (photo – Mike Sudds)

A GMC K30FC Rescue Tender bodied by Woodways was built in 1988 for Dogsthorpe and 1989 saw the introduction of two Prime Movers on the Volvo FL614 chassis and fitted with Multilift lifting equipment.

Two Pods were built by Fulton & Wylie; an Incident Command & Control Unit and a Special Rescue Unit. Although the original intention was to build a

1987 Bedford TKM 4×4/JDC Water Carrier D750 KVA (photo – David Palmer)

1986 Ford Transit Chemical Incident Unit and Trailer C643 KCE (photo – Pete Ashpool)

Kimbolton Fire station personnel 1987 (Back row l. to r. Fm. Colman, Fm. Small, Fm. Gooderham, Fm. Mehew, Fm. Blackman. Front row l. to r. Fm. Rowland, L/Fm. Sansom, Sub O. Stapleton, L/Fm. Stewart, L/Fm Woodham) (photo – Kimbolton Fire Station)

1988 GMC K30FC/Woodway Rescue Tender D940 EEW (photo – Gordon Townsend collection)

whole series of pods, the concept was not as successful as first thought and no further ones were built.

1991 saw a Mercedes 1120AF 4×4 Special Rescue Unit fitted with equipment lockers designed by Rosenbauer, an Austrian company, supplied to Huntingdon. This appliance replaced the Pod Unit which was converted to an Operational Support Unit. The same year also saw a Carmichael bodied Mercedes 811D Rescue Tender being built for Dogsthorpe.

Concerns had been raised that in the event of a major incident in a remote area, e.g. a train crash or aircraft incident, access could be difficult for the Incident Control Unit and other appliances. Therefore in 1992 a Land Rover Defender was purchased and fitted out as a Forward Control Unit. It could also be used to ferry crews and equipment across rough terrain.

In 1992 one of the Prime Movers was converted to a Hazardous Substances Rescue Unit by removing the Multilift equipment, lengthening the chassis, adding a HIAB crane and fitting additional bodywork by JDC. This appliance then replaced the Chemical Incident Unit at St Neots.

The early 1990s also saw the amalgamation of the two workshop facilities at Cambridge and Dogsthorpe into one unit at Dogsthorpe. The Huntingdon workshop had already been closed in the early days of the Fire & Rescue Service.

1993 saw the concept of Rescue Tenders change when a Rescue/Damage Control Unit was built by Angloco on a Mercedes 1124AF chassis and based at Cambridge.

1989 Volvo FL614/Multilift F611 BAV with Incident Control Unit Pod (photo – Author's collection)

1989 Volvo FL614/Multilift Prime Mover F612 BAV with Special Rescue Unit Pod (photo – Pete Ashpool)

St Neots Fire Station personnel 1990 (photo – Author's collection)

1991 Mercedes 1120AF 4×4/ Rosenbauer Special Rescue Unit H151 JFL (photo – Mike Sudds)

1991 Mercedes 811D/Carmichael Rescue Tender H410 CEW (photo – Gordon Townsend collection)

Volvo FL614/HIAB/JDC Hazardous Substances Rescue Unit F612 BAV (photo – Mike Sudds)

In 1995 came the introduction of two new special appliances for Hunting-don. The first was a Water/Foam Unit on a 6×4 Mercedes 2531 chassis with bodywork by Carmichaels. The other was an Operational Support Unit (OSU) on a Mercedes 814D chassis and bodied by Gladwins, a local bodybuilder. It was designed in three sections; the front section carries 40 BA cylinders and also has an area for servicing BA sets, the middle section is a storage area for folding tables and chairs, food packs, fresh water supplies and also carries a Hi-expansion Foam unit; the rear section is a kitchen area which serves hot meals and drinks. The OSU is mobilised to all six-pump fires and above and can also be requested at other incidents by the officer in charge.

In 1996 the first Dennis TSD203 Sabre fire appliance was introduced to the fleet and over the next three years eighteen Water Tender Ladders on this chassis had been built all by JDC.

1997 saw the last of the pod units disposed of when a Mercedes 817 Incident Control Unit, with bodywork by Excalibur, went on the run at Huntingdon. Designed in three sections, it has a radio room, a command centre and a conference room. The Incident Control Unit is mobilised to incidents requiring five pumps or above.

Two Turntable Ladders on the MAN M2000 chassis were supplied in 1999 and 2000, built by GB Fire with 100 ft articulated ladders for Dogsthorpe and Cambridge. These ladders are different from standard turntable ladders in that the top section is 'hinged' and allows the ladder to be used in an 'up and over' mode similar to a hydraulic platform. The MAN L2000 chassis was used in 1999 for the supply of a Community Fire Safety Vehicle built by JDC. The same chassis and bodybuilder combination were used when three Rescue Vehicles were purchased in 1999, 2001 and 2002. These three appliances, based at Cambridge, Dogsthorpe and Huntingdon have been standardised and now all carry the same equipment, including inflatable boats and inflatable paths, whereas their predecessors were each designed for specific roles.

Wisbech Fire Station personnel c.2000 (photo – George Dunlop collection)

'Old and New' at Huntingdon Fire Station – 2004 Scania P94D-260/Emergency – One Water Tender Ladder KX53 FJZ (wholetime) and 1992 Dennis RS237/JDC Water Tender Ladder J988 TEG (retained) in foreground (photo – David Palmer)

In 2001 the service's long association with Dennis fire appliances came to an end when for the first time a Scania P94D-260 Water Tender Ladder was built by JDC. In total, this combination was used to supply a further eight appliances.

In 2003 a MAN LE280B 4×4 chassis with bodywork by Massey Tankers was used for the supply of a Water Carrier for Yaxley replacing the last Bedford appliance in the fleet. In 2004 a further three Water Tender Ladders on the Scania chassis were purchased, but this time the bodybuilders Emergency One were used for the first time. A further three were supplied in 2005 with three more due in 2006.

Following legislation changing the method of dealing with hazardous incidents, and taking into account the age of the vehicle, it was decided to replace the Hazardous Substances Rescue Unit, at St Neots, with a different concept of appliance. A Mercedes Vario 814D van fitted out by Emergency One was built in 2004 and went on the run as a Hazardous Materials Unit. This is the third different type of appliance each with a different appliance designation to carry out the role since 1986.

Another new appliance delivered in 2004 was an Incident Response Unit (IRU) supplied from the Government's New Dimensions Program, which carries equipment capable of the mass decontamination of up to 400 people per hour. These appliances also carry equipment for the use of firefighters such as gas tight suits, detection and monitoring equipment. When mobilised, the IRU is

'Changing Faces' at St Neots Fire Station – 2004 Mercedes Vario 814D/ Emergency One Hazardous Materials Unit AE04 FVH and 1989 Volvo FL614/HIAB/JDC Hazardous Substances Rescue Unit F612 BAV (photo – Mike Sudds)

supported by eight pumps from local stations whose crews have been trained to use the specialist equipment.

Another vehicle which has arrived in the brigade from New Dimensions is a High Volume Pumping Unit (HVPU). This consists of a prime mover with a pod unit carrying the high volume pump and 1 km of 150 mm hose. A second unit carrying 2 km of hose is due in May 2006 and later in the year a Mass Decontamination Disrobe Unit is due in the brigade. The Disrobe Unit will carry replacement packs for the Incident Response Unit in the case of a protracted incident.

The Service's Training Department is based at Huntingdon Fire Station, where a Fire Training House and Breathing Apparatus complex was built in 1992. Wholetime recruit training courses are carried out by other brigades, currently West Midlands Fire and Rescue Service, but continuation training is carried out internally. All retained training, including recruit courses, is carried out at the Huntingdon Training Centre.

A self-contained extension to St Ives Fire Station was built in 1994, including accommodation for personnel attending courses at the nearby Huntingdon Training Centre. The building also contains the Occupational Health Unit.

Since Fire Control moved into the new Control Suite in 1986 there have been many changes and upgrades to the mobilising equipment and with the current computer system it is now possible for Control Operators to direct crews to specific locations by the use of mapping systems.

Training course waiting to enter the fire house for a BA exercise (photo – Mike Sudds)

Fire Control at Headquarters (photo – the Author)

The Fire Safety Department had been based at Cambridge Fire Station with local offices based at Peterborough and Huntingdon. However, during 2003 the Service was restructured and aligned itself with the six district/city council boundaries. This restructure is enabling the Service to identify local needs, support local activities and become more involved with community safety groups and Local Strategic Partnerships that currently operate within district and city council boundaries.

Since the 1st April 2003 the Service has been under the control of the Cambridgeshire and Peterborough Fire Authority. The Fire Authority came into existence following yet another re-organisation of local government in Cambridgeshire and the creation of a separate unitary authority for Peterborough. The costs of the Fire Authority are met by the Cambridgeshire County and the Peterborough City Councils but the Fire Authority is a separate legal and organisational entity.

The six Service Districts are Cambridge City, East Cambridgeshire, Fenland, Huntingdonshire, Peterborough City and South Cambridgeshire each being under the control of a Divisional Officer. The emergency response arrangements have not changed but the Service is now better able to establish local contacts to deliver fire safety advice and initiatives. The Cambridgeshire Fire and Rescue Service is responsible for delivering Fire and Rescue Services to an area of over 1,300 square miles with a population in excess of 740,000 people from 28 Fire Stations, Fire Control and the 6 District Offices. The Service employs 650 firefighters who deal with over 12,000 separate incidents each year.

The main urban areas within the county include Peterborough, Cambridge, St Neots, Huntingdon, Wisbech and St Ives. The area contains a diversity of risks including the cathedrals of Ely and Peterborough, the historic buildings of Cambridge University and the high-tech industries of the 'Silicon Fen' around Cambridge. There are four large hospitals in the county; Addenbrookes in Cambridge, Hinchingbrooke in Huntingdon, the Peterborough District Hospital and the world famous heart hospital at Papworth. In addition to the agricultural industries of rural Cambridgeshire, there are also pockets of heavy industry in Peterborough. With the county being criss- crossed by a number of main routes, including the M11, A1(M), A1, A10, A14 and the A47 trunk roads, the Service is called upon to deal with many hazardous and dangerous incidents on a daily basis. Two Inter-City rail lines from London run through the county and there are a number of airfields, both civil and military, including the Imperial War Museum at Duxford with its inherent high risk on flying days, so fire crews regularly practise to deal with major incidents. The Service is also well equipped to deal with flooding and river incidents which are common in the low-lying fens.

With continuing improvements and maintenance to the service's premises every station now has exhaust extraction units for each appliance and facilities for female firefighters including separate showers.

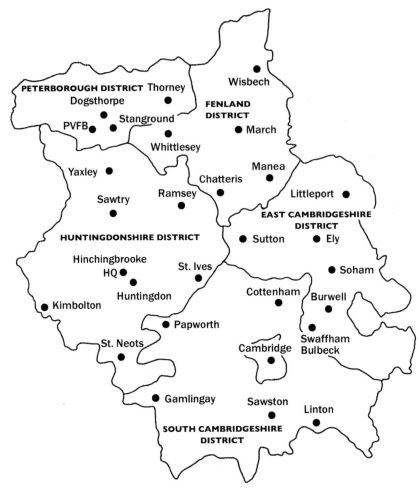

Cambridgeshire Fire & Rescue Service 2005

There are proposals for the redevelopment of the Parkside Fire Station site in Cambridge. The Fire and Rescue Service's plans for this redevelopment have been based on the need for modernisation of the site and puts the fire station at the centre of the regeneration of the site. Built above the four-bay fire station will be approximately 130 residential flats and the Service hopes to obtain ten of these for staff. Other key worker and affordable housing will also be available. During construction, Cambridge firefighters will operate from a temporary fire station at the Territorial Army Barracks in Coldham Lane, Cambridge.

The City of Peterborough also has a very unique fire station; the Peterborough Volunteer Fire Brigade which is in effect a private Fire Brigade contracted to the Cambridgeshire Fire & Rescue Service to provide twenty-four hour fire cover. The Brigade, the only one of its kind in the UK, receives an annual fee from the Fire Authority but all of the members give their services completely free of charge. The City Centre Fire Station is owned by the PVFB, has its own administration, but otherwise conforms to the standards, procedures and training of a conventional retained fire station.

A major change to the service is currently taking place, along with all the other Fire & Rescue Services, the use of ranks are being removed and replaced with national role definitions. The following chart shows the planned changes:

Old rank	New role definition	Identification
Firefighter	Firefighter	Yellow helmet
Leading Firefighter	Crew Manager	Yellow helmet with 2×12.5 mm black bands
Sub Officer	Watch Manager A and B★	White helmet with 1×12.5 mm black band
Station Officer Assistant Divisional Officer	Station Manager A and B★	White helmet with 1×19 mm black band
Assistant Divisional Officer Divisional Officer II	Group Manager	White helmet with 1×19 mm and 1×12.5 mm black bands
Divisional Officer I Senior Divisional Officer	Area Manager	White helmet with 2×19 mm black bands
Assistant Chief Officer Deputy Chief Officer Chief Fire Officer	Brigade Manager	White helmet with 1×38 mm black band

★ Dependent of size of station

THE Chief Fire Officer's responsibilities are partly delegated by the fire authority and are partly statutory as set up by central government. Within the framework of the establishment scheme, approved policies, the nationally recommended standard of fire cover and the resources made available to him, the Chief Fire Officer is responsible to the fire authority for the efficient operation of the Fire and Rescue Service. To assist him in his duties, the Chief Fire Officer has a Deputy Chief Fire Officer and a number of Assistant Chief Fire Officers, who each have specific roles.

1974 to 1978 – John C. Maxwell, O.B.E., D.F.C. (Bar), Q.F.S.M.

When the Cambridgeshire Fire & Rescue Service was formed on the 1st April 1974 its first Chief Fire Officer was John C. Maxwell, former Chief Fire Officer of the Huntingdon & Peterborough County Fire Service. John became an operational fireman when war broke out in 1939 and then joined the RAF in 1940. After wartime service, flying bombers and winning the Distinguished Flying Cross and Bar, he rejoined the fire service in his native Scotland, later moving to Hertfordshire and then Suffolk following various promotions. He was promoted to Chief Fire Officer of Huntingdon and Peterborough County Fire Service in 1969 and then on amalgamation became Chief Officer of the new Cambridgeshire Fire & Rescue Service. In 1978 John announced his retirement and took up a post as Assistant Commandant at the Fire Service College, Moreton-in-Marsh. Sadly John died in hospital from injuries suffered in a road traffic accident in June 1989.

1978 to 1987 – Duncan McCallum, O.B.E., M.I.Fire E.

Following John Maxwell's retirement, Duncan McCallum was appointed to take his place. Duncan had joined the Glasgow Fire Service in 1957 where he rose to the rank of Station Officer. He transferred to Cheshire in 1968, where he rose to the rank of Divisional Officer before transferring to Essex as a Divisional Commander in 1972. In 1975 he was appointed ACO of Norfolk Fire Service before returning to Essex as Deputy Chief Officer in 1977. Duncan retired in 1987 and took up a position with Her Majesty's Fire Services Inspectorate.

1987 to 2000 – Alan Gray, O.B.E., G.I.Fire E.

Alan Gray joined the London Fire Brigade in 1965 and was promoted through the ranks, apart from a period of secondment at the Fire Service College, to the position of Chief Staff Office in 1983. Alan was appointed Deputy Chief Officer of Cambridgeshire in 1985 and when Duncan McCallum retired in 1987 Alan was appointed Chief Fire Officer. He announced his retirement in 2000.

2001 onwards – Tom Carroll, Q.F.S.M., M.I.Fire E.

Tom Carroll joined the fire service in Cambridgeshire in 1977 and worked his way through the ranks to the position of Assistant Divisional Officer by 1991. After service in Northumberland as a Divisional Officer he was appointed Deputy Chief Fire Officer in Oxfordshire in 1995. In 1997 he was promoted to Chief Fire Officer before moving back to Cambridgeshire in 2001 to become its fourth Chief Fire Officer. In 2005 Tom was elected President of the Chief Fire Officers Association, the first Cambridge-shire Chief Fire Officer to have the honour of holding this post.

A14   Dogsthorpe

Dogsthorpe Fire Station – opened 1964 (photo – Karl Sillitoe)

Address: Dogsthorpe Road, Peterborough, PE1 3RE.
Duty System: Wholetime (24 hour).
Appliances: 1 Water Tender Ladder, 1 Turntable Ladder, 1 Rescue
                Vehicle.

A15   Peterborough Volunteer Fire Brigade

PVFB Fire Station – opened 1982 (photo – Author's collection)

Address: Bourges Boulevard, Peterborough, PE1 1AF.
Duty System: Volunteer.
Appliances: 2 Water Tender Ladders.

A16   Stanground

Stanground Fire Station – opened 1977 (photo – Author's collection)

Address: Belle Vue, Stanground, PE2 8RA.
Duty System: Wholetime (24 hour).
Appliances: 1 Water Tender Ladder, 1 Incident Response Unit.

A17   Yaxley

Yaxley Fire Station – opened 1887, extended 1965 (photo – Author's collection)

Address: Main Street, Yaxley, PE7 3LB.
Duty System: Retained.
Appliances: 1 Water Tender Ladder, 1 Water Carrier.

A18   Whittlesey

Whittlesey Fire Station – opened 1967 (photo – The author)

Address: Cemetery Road, Whittlesey, PE7 1RU.
Duty System: Retained.
Appliances: 1 Water Tender Ladder, 1 Red Cross Fire Victim Support
                 Unit.

A19   Thorney

Thorney Fire Station – opened 1972 (photo – The author)

Address: Tank Yard, Station Road, Thorney, PE6 0QE.
Duty System: Retained.
Appliances: 1 Water Tender Ladder.

A20   Wisbech

Wisbech Fire Station – opened 1987 (photo – Gordon Townsend collection)

Address: Churchill Road, Wisbech, PE13 2DN.
Duty System: Day manning (7 day) with retained backup.
Appliances: 2 Water Tender Ladders.

A21   March

March Fire Station – opened 1963 (photo – Karl Sillitoe)

Address: Wisbech Road, March, PE15 8ED.
Duty System: Retained.
Appliances: 2 Water Tender Ladders, 1 Operational Support Unit

A22   Manea

Manea Fire Station – opened 1978 (photo – David Palmer)

Address: Westfield Road, Manea, PE15 0LN.
Duty System: Retained.
Appliances: 1 Water Tender Ladder.

A23   Chatteris

Chatteris Fire Station – opened 1956 (photo – Karl Sillitoe)

Address: Station Street, Chatteris, PE16 6NA.
Duty System: Retained.
Appliances: 1 Water Tender Ladder.

A24   Ramsey

Ramsey Fire Station – opened 1962 (photo – The author)

Address: Great Whyte, Ramsey, PE26 1HS.
Duty System: Retained.
Appliances: 2 Water Tender Ladders.

A25   Sawtry

Sawtry Fire Station – opened 1966 (photo – Author's collection)

Address: Green End Road, Sawtry, PE28 5UX.
Duty System: Retained.
Appliances: 1 Water Tender Ladder.

A26   Kimbolton

Kimbolton Fire Station – opened 1958 (photo – The author)

Address: Thrapston Road, Kimbolton, PE28 0HW.
Duty System: Retained.
Appliances: 1 Water Tender Ladder.

A27   Huntingdon

Huntingdon Fire Station – opened 1967 (photo – The author)

Address: Hartford Road, Huntingdon, PE29 3RH.
Duty System: Wholetime (24 hour) with retained backup.
Appliances: 2 Water Tender Ladders, 1 Rescue Vehicle, 1 Water Foam
                  Unit, 1 Incident Command Unit, 1 High Volume Pumping
                  Unit.

A28 St Ives

St Ives Fire Station – opened 1971 (photo – Author's collection)

Address: Ramsey Road, St Ives, PE27 5RA.
Duty System: Retained.
Appliances: 2 Water Tender Ladders.

B01 Cambridge

Cambridge Fire Station – opened 1965 (photo – Author's collection)

Address: Parkside, Cambridge, CB1 1JE.
Duty System: Wholetime (24 hour).
Appliances: 2 Water Tender Ladders, 1 Turntable Ladder, 1 Rescue
 Vehicle.

B02   Cottenham

Cottenham Fire Station – opened 1961 (photo – The author)

Address: High Street, Cottenham, CB4 8RX.
Duty System: Retained.
Appliances: 1 Water Tender Ladder.

B03   Sutton

Sutton Fire Station – opened 1960 (photo – Karl Sillitoe)

Address: Mepal Road, Sutton, CB6 2PZ.
Duty System: Retained.
Appliances: 1 Water Tender Ladder.

B04   Littleport

Littleport Fire Station – opened 1965 (photo – Karl Sillitoe)

Address: Ponts Hill, Littleport, CB6 1PZ.
Duty System: Retained.
Appliances: 1 Water Tender Ladder.

B05   Ely

Ely Fire Station – opened 1970 (photo – Karl Sillitoe)

Address: Egremont Street, Ely, CB6 1AE.
Duty System: Day manning (5 day) with retained backup.
Appliances: 2 Water Tender Ladders.

B06   Soham

Soham Fire Station – opened 1954 (photo – David Palmer)

Address: Fountain Lane, Soham, CB7 5ED.
Duty System: Retained.
Appliances: 2 Water Tender Ladders.

B07   Burwell

Burwell Fire Station – opened 1978 (ex Works Fire Brigade) (photo – David Palmer)

Address: Scotred Lane, Burwell, CB5 0AL.
Duty System: Retained.
Appliances: 1 Water Tender Ladder.

B08   Swaffham Bulbeck

Swaffham Bulbeck Fire Station – opened 1938 (converted from 18th century barn) (photo – David Palmer)

Address: High Street, Swaffham Bulbeck, CB5 0LX.
Duty System: Retained.
Appliances: 1 Water Tender Ladder.

B09   Linton

Linton Fire Station – opened 1954 (photo – The author)

Address: Balsham Road, Linton, CB1 6LE.
Duty System: Retained.
Appliances: 1 Water Tender Ladder.

B10   Sawston

Sawston Fire Station – opened 1971 (photo – Author's collection)

Address: Mill Lane, Sawston, CB2 4HY.
Duty System: Retained.
Appliances: 1 Water Tender Ladder.

B11   Gamlingay

Gamlingay Fire Station – opened 1966 (photo – The author)

Address: Stocks Lane, Gamlingay, SG19 3JP.
Duty System: Retained.
Appliances: 1 Water Tender Ladder.

B12   Papworth Everard

Papworth Everard Fire Station – opened 1961 (photo – Karl Sillitoe)

Address: Ermine Street, Papworth Everard, CB3 8RH.
Duty System: Retained.
Appliances: 1 Water Tender Ladder.

B13   St Neots

St Neots Fire Station – opened 1968 (photo – Karl Sillitoe)

Address: Huntingdon Street, St Neots, PE19 1DU.
Duty System: Day manning (5 day) with retained backup.
Appliances: 2 Water Tender Ladders, 1 Hazardous Materials Unit.

Dennis RS241/JDC Water Tender Ladder M848 GEG (photo – Karl Sillitoe)

Dennis Sabre/JDC Water Tender Ladder N490 SAV (photo – Karl Sillitoe)

Scania P94D-260/JDC Water Tender Ladder AF02 XTL (photo – Mike Sudds)

Scania P94D-260/Emergency One Water Tender Ladder KX53 FJZ (photo – David Palmer)

MAN M2000/GB Fire/Magirus Turntable Ladder T837 RFL (photo – Karl Sillitoe)

MAN L2000/JDC Rescue Vehicle T838 RFL (photo – David Palmer)

MAN L2000/JDC Rescue Vehicle Y724 WVA (photo – Mike Sudds)

Mercedes Vario 814D/Emergency One Hazardous Materials Unit AE04 FVH (photo – Mike Sudds)

Mercedes 2531 6×4/Carmichael/Dennis Eagle Water Foam Unit L140 VCE (photo – David Palmer)

Man LE280B 4×4/Massey Tankers Water Carrier AF52 VMM (photo – Mike Sudds)

Mercedes 817/Excalibur Incident Control Unit R615 TAV (photo – Mike Sudds)

Mercedes 814D/Excalibur Operational Support Unit L452 TFL (photo – Mike Sudds)

MAN TGA 6x2/Marshalls SV Incident Response Unit DG53 FZL (photo – The author)

Moffett Mounty Fork Lift fitted to rear of Incident Response Unit DG53 FZL (photo – The author)

MAN TGA 6×2/Marshalls SV Heavy Volume Pumping Unit WX54 VMJ (photo – The author)

June 1976 – near Thorney. A US Air Force C141 Starlifter Cargo Jet, with eighteen passengers on board, was on a routine flight from New Jersey to RAF Mildenhall in Suffolk, when it crashed during a sudden and violent thunderstorm. On the arrival of the first crew from Thorney there was little visible of the aircraft, which had buried itself in the ground leaving mainly the wings and tailplane showing. The fire was extinguished and on arrival of supporting crews a search was made of the area in case anyone had been thrown clear but no survivors were found, only part of a wing some distance away.

3rd May 1977 – Huntingdon. At 12.13 hours, just before local schools let out pupils for their lunch break, a Canberra photo-reconnaissance aircraft, returning from Scotland to RAF Wyton, crashed into a row of terraced houses in Norfolk Road with devastating consequences. The crew of two and three young children trapped in their homes were killed and a further six people injured. Firefighting crews from the nearby airfield were on the scene within 5 minutes plus crews from Huntingdon and other local fire stations and found eight homes totally destroyed. Police had to form a cordon to hold back hundreds of sightseers.

Huntingdon plane crash, 1977 (photo – *Hunts. Post*)

Wisbech plane crash, 1979 (photo – *Wisbech Standard*)

September 1979 – Wisbech. Two Harrier jump jets from the Royal Air Force collided over the town of Wisbech. Both pilots ejected safely but one of the planes crashed into Ramnoth Road. One bungalow was completely destroyed killing one of the occupants. In a pair of adjacent houses, which were virtually destroyed, a 2½ year old boy and his father were also killed. A further seven persons were injured. Crews and appliances from Cambridgeshire, Norfolk and Lincolnshire attended this harrowing incident.

1983 – Timber yard, Eynesbury. In the early hours, two appliances from St Neots were mobilised to a fire in the timber yard of C. G. Tebbutt, St Marys Street, Eynesbury. Retained crews responding from their homes had seen the extent of the fire and an immediate message '*make pumps 4*' was sent on booking mobile to the incident. On arrival, the number of pumps required for this incident was increased to six. Additional crews from Huntingdon plus the RV/CU, Gamlingay, Kimbolton and Papworth responded. Despite efforts from the crews the saw mill and timber storage sheds were destroyed.

The saw mill as seen on arrival, C. G. Tebbutts, Eynesbury (photo – Author's collection)

Fighting the timber yard fire, Eynesbury (photo – Author's collection)

23rd January 1984 – Cottenham. At 20.35 hours pumps from Cottenham and Cambridge were sent to a reported fire in a toy manufacturing factory in the village. The building, 18 metres by 34 metres, used as a store for insulation materials, was found to be well alight and reinforcements were called from Cambridge (2nd pump, Turntable Ladder, Rescue Tender and Water Carrier), Sutton, Swaffham Bulbeck, Ely and the RV/CU from Huntingdon. Six jets and six BA were used to extinguish the fire, which severely damaged 95 per cent of the building and its contents.

Sunday, 26th August 1984 – *City Limits*, Station Road, Cambridge. An arsonist struck on a peaceful Bank Holiday Sunday lunchtime, when crews from Cambridge were called to the *City Limits* nightclub. The ground floor night-club and student accommodation on the two floors above were well alight

City Limits nightclub, Cambridge, 1984 (photo – Geoff Heathcock)

when crews arrived and there were initial fears that people may have been trapped. A search of the building by BA teams fortunately found the building clear, but found empty fuel cans and a strong smell of paraffin on all floors. Fruit machines had also been broken into. Damage was estimated at £250,000.

Wednesday, 23rd October 1985 – RAF Brampton. At 21.22 hours fire control was alerted to a fire at RAF Support Command Headquarters. Two pumps from Huntingdon were mobilised and immediately after booking in attendance sent a message '*make pumps 4*'. At 21.44 hours a further message '*make pumps 6, TL required*' was sent followed at 22.07 hours by '*make pumps 10 for water relay*'. A further make-up message was sent at 22.22 hours '*make pumps 15, TLs 2*' followed at 22.45 hours by '*make pumps 20, 2 water carriers required*' and by midnight pumps from Huntingdon (2), St Neots, St Ives (2), Ramsey (2), Kimbolton, Papworth, Sawtry, Stanground, Cambridge, Yaxley, March, PVFB, Sutton, Gamlingay, Thrapston (Northants) and Sandy (Bedfordshire) were in attendance. The Turntable Ladders from both Cambridge and Dogsthorpe, the RV/CU from Huntingdon, the RV from Cambridge and the Water Carriers from Yaxley and Wisbech completed the attendance. The building of three floors, 100 metres by 40 metres was severely damaged and twelve jets, two turntable monitors, Stage II BA and a water relay were used to extinguish the fire. Relief crews were in attendance until the evening of the 26th October.

RAF Brampton – the blaze at its height (photo – Gordon Depledge collection)

10th May 1986 – Chapter House, Leverington, Wisbech. Two pumps were mobilised from Wisbech at 23.20 hours to a fire in a large detached house of three storeys. On arrival a '*make pumps 4*' message was sent and appliances from Long Sutton (Lincolnshire) and West Walton (Norfolk) were sent on plus the Water Carrier from Wisbech and the Control Unit from Huntingdon. A '*make pumps 6*' message brought on March and Outwell (Norfolk). The stop message of '*Ground, 1st and 2nd floors well alight, 5 jets and water relay in use*' was timed at 00.16 hours and the cause was given as of '*doubtful origin*'.

22nd March 1989 – Fengate, Peterborough. This day will always be remembered with great sadness by the Fire & Rescue Service in Cambridge-shire. On the receipt of the initial call, two pumping appliances and a Rescue Tender from Stanground and Dogsthorpe fire stations were mobilised to a '*tanker on fire*' at the Vibroplant depot. Soon after the appliances booked in attendance there was a huge explosion, which spread debris around the area. By the time reinforcing crews had arrived on the scene, one firefighter, John Humphries, had been killed in the explosion and several others were seriously injured. Stanground's pump was badly damaged and Dogsthorpe's Rescue Tender was damaged so severely that it had to be written off. Many surrounding buildings were also heavily damaged. The injured were soon taken into ambulances and transferred to hospital. By now it had been established that the information on the original 999 call was tragically incorrect. It was not a tanker

The damaged fire appliances, Fengate, Peterborough (photo – *Peterborough Evening Telegraph*)

that was involved but an unmarked van carrying explosives and detonators that had caught fire and exploded in Vibroplant's yard. A thorough search was made of all the damaged buildings and the surrounding area and no further casualties were found. The following week a full Fire Service Funeral was held for John Humphries, which was attended by firefighters from all over the UK including many of his colleagues still suffering from their injuries caused by the explosion.

3rd September 1989 – Brook End Farm, Catworth. A typical farm fire occurred in a dutch barn containing many tons of baled straw. Pumping appliances from Kimbolton, Huntingdon, Sawtry and Thrapston (Northants.) attended plus the Water Carrier from Yaxley. The priorities of crews was to protect other nearby farm buildings.

26th July 1990 – High Street, Burwell. At 05.40 hours crews from Burwell and Swaffham Bulbeck were sent to The Maltings where a serious fire was in progress. The building, a recently restored picturesque thatched barn and oast house, containing a small business complex was engulfed in flames. Nearby houses were evacuated and reinforcements were requested and in total six pumps plus specialist appliances were in attendance and twenty-four BA sets, three jets

Fire at Brooke End Farm, Catworth, 1989 (photo – Kimbolton Fire Station)

Fire at Burwell Maltings, 1990 (photo – Geoff Heathcock)

and six hosereels were used to extinguish the blaze. The fire which took four hours to bring under control caused havoc to commuter traffic travelling from nearby villages to Cambridge and caused an estimated £250,000 of damage.

17th December 1991 – St Ivo School, High Leys, St Ives. At 00.44 hours two pumps from St Ives were sent to a reported fire in the school science block. On arrival, a severe fire was found to be in progress and further appliances were requested. In total 8 pumps were in attendance from St Ives (2), Huntingdon (2), Ramsey (2), Papworth and Sutton. The TL (Cambridge) and the WrC and ICU (both Huntingdon) made up the attendance. The stop message at 04.05 hours stated '*Building used as school science block, 50m by 50m, 90% severely damaged by fire, 6 jets, 1 TL monitor, 18 BA, hydrants and open water in use*'.

26th February 1992 – A14, Molesworth. The newly opened A1/M1 Link Road was the scene of a fatal road traffic accident, when a collision occurred between a car and a lorry at a farm crossing on the westbound carriageway. Both vehicles were severely damaged in the fire which followed. Pumps from Kimbolton and Thrapston (Northants) attended plus the Rescue Vehicle from Huntingdon.

6th March 1992 – Stonewell Cottage, Church Lane, Stibbington. Three appliances from Stanground, Yaxley and Dogsthorpe were mobilised at 10.00 hours to a fire in a thatched cottage. On arrival a '*make pumps 6, water carrier required*' message was sent and additional appliances from PVFB (2) and

Road traffic accident, A14 Molesworth, 1992 (photo – Kimbolton Fire Station)

Stamford (Lincs) were sent on to the incident. Also mobilised were the WrC (Yaxley), RT (Dogsthorpe), ICU and OSU (both from Huntingdon). The stop message sent at 11.36 hours was as follows '*Detached building, 20 metres by 11 metres, thatched and tiled roof, 2 jets, 4 hosereels, 4 BA*'.

26th April 1993 – Gates Hydraulics, Station Road, St Neots. A serious fire broke at 20.16 hours in a factory building 150 metres by 50 metres. A total of six pumping appliances from St Neots (2), Huntingdon, Gamlingay, Kimbolton and Sandy (Bedfordshire) attended and fourteen BA sets, two jets and five hosereels were used to extinguish the fire. The TL (Cambridge), ICU (Huntingdon) and HSRU (St Neots) were also in attendance. A number of cylinders were removed from the premises and cooled down.

28th April 1993 – Derelict school, Huntingdon. In the early afternoon fire control received a call to a fire in the old Hinchingbrooke Lower School. Two pumps from Huntingdon responded together with a duty officer from Brigade Headquarters just across the road. On arrival the officer sent an assistance message '*make pumps 6, turntable ladder required*'. St Neots (2), St Ives and Papworth Everard were sent together with the ICU (Huntingdon) and TL (Cambridge). A further assistance message '*make pumps 10, TLs 2*' brought on

Hinchingbrooke School, 1993 (photo – *Hunts. Post*)

Ramsey (2), Sawtry, Kimbolton and Dogsthorpe (TL). The fire which was started deliberately was first spotted through the roof of the main hall and when high winds got to grips the fire spread rapidly. The stop message was sent at 17.25 hours with twelve BA and six jets in use.

June 1993 – A1 Trunk Road, Wittering. Firefighters from the Peterborough area attended a heavy goods vehicle leaking nitric acid on the southbound carriageway of the A1 near RAF Wittering. There was a danger of the acid coming into contact with sodium hydrosulphite carried in another container on the vehicle. Eventually some 155 gallons (700 litres) of nitric acid had to be decanted into a container on another lorry. A total of eighteen BA sets, two gas-tight suits, six chemical protection suits and a decontamination shower were used. The A1 was closed for most of the day and major traffic jams built up. Luckily there were no injuries but firefighters spent some seven hours on this taxing job.

22nd May 1994 – St Marys School, Wintringham Road, St Neots. At 02.52 hours two appliances from St Neots were mobilised to a fire at the above address. On arrival, a serious fire was in progress and a '*make pumps 4*' message brought on pumps from Gamlingay and Kimbolton plus the Incident Control Unit from Huntingdon. At 03.14 hours a further make-up message was sent '*make pumps 6, turntable ladder and water carrier required*'. On receiving this message Fire Control ordered on pumps from Huntingdon and Papworth, the Turntable Ladder from Dogsthorpe and the Water Carrier from Huntingdon.

Interior of St Mary's School, 1994 (photo – *Hunts. Post*)

This was followed by an informative message '*Primary school, single storey traditional structure, 50 metres by 50 metres, 100% of roof well alight, 2 jets, 4 BA*'. Another make-up message was sent at 03.40 hours '*Make pumps 10 for water relay, shortage of water*'. This brought on Huntingdon's second pump, St Ives and Sandy and Potton, both from Bedfordshire. Cambridge's Rescue Unit attended to assist with salvage and the Hazardous Substances Unit from St Neots attended to remove chemicals from the swimming pool area. The stop message was sent at 06.06 hours detailing '*Fire in school, 8 jets, TL monitor, 24 BA, 2 hydrants, 4 pump relay from open water*'.

11th January 1995 – Old Passport Office, Peterborough. At 20.57 hours a call was received to a fire in an empty office building. Appliances attending were from Dogsthope (WrL & TL), Stanground (WrL), PVFB (2 WrL), Yaxley (WrL), March (WrL), Ramsey (WrL), Sawtry (WrL), Cambridge (TL), Huntingdon (ICU & OSU). Lincolnshire provided two WrLs from Crowland and Market Deeping. The fire involved a two-storey office building, 20 metres by 20 metres and six jets, four hosereels, two TL monitors and six BA were used to extinguish the fire.

28th October 1995 – Gates Hydraulics, Station Road, St Neots. It has been said many times that lighting does not strike twice but fire can, and frequently does. The Fire & Rescue Service were called at 03.00 hours to a fire almost 18 months to the day from the last fire in the same building in April 1993. Two pumps and the Hazardous Substances Unit from St Neots were

Gates Hydraulics, 'the morning after' (photo – Kimbolton Fire Station)

mobilised as the call indicated that chemicals were possibly involved. Soon after arrival a '*make pumps 4 for BA*' message was sent and Gamlingay, Kimbolton and the Incident Control Unit from Huntingdon were mobilised. Further make-ups for a '*rescue unit for gas-tight suits*' and then '*make pumps 6, turntable ladder required*' were sent. These brought on Papworth, Huntingdon, the Rescue Unit from Huntingdon and the Turntable Ladder from Cambridge. At 03.35 hours a message stating that '*the fire was in the roof and a flashover had occurred*' followed immediately by a message '*make rescue units 2*' and then '*make pumps 10*'. Pumps from Sawtry and the Ops Support Unit from Huntingdon plus three pumps from Bedfordshire; Sandy, Potton and Bedford were sent. Following a message at 04.03 hours '*make pumps 15, turntable ladders 2*', pumps from Ramsey (2), St Ives (2) and Cambridge plus the Turntable Ladder from Dogsthorpe were sent. Another make-up message was sent 04.18 hours '*make pumps 20 for water relay*'. This brought on Cottenham, Yaxley, Stanground, Chatteris and Ampthill (Bedfordshire). The stop message was sent at 12.42 hours detailing '*fire in factory unit, 200 metres by 50 metres, used for hydraulic production and equipment, 70% of the building severely damaged by fire, numerous BA, 12 jets, 2 TL monitors, 2 ground monitors in use; AFFF, water relay*'. The water relay was from the River Great Ouse, 1½ miles away.

2nd March 1997 – Incinerco, Eaton Socon. This incident involved 15 tonnes of clinical waste in an enclosed yard adjacent to two factory units. Four jets, one ground monitor, fifteen chemical protection suits, twenty-five BA, full decontamination procedures plus two hydrants were used by crews from St Neots (2 plus HSRU), Gamlingay, Kimbolton, Papworth Everard, Huntingdon (RV, ICU and OSU).

2nd March 1997 – *Old Ferry Boat Inn*, Holywell. The fire involved the thatched roof of this period building, 30 metres by 30 metres, of two floors and irregular shape, used as a public house and hotel. Approximately 50 per cent of the roof and first floor were severely damaged and fifty BA, ten jets, TL monitor and a water relay from the nearby River Ouse were used. The following crews attended: St Ives (2), Huntingdon (2), Papworth Everard, Ramsey (2), Chatteris, March, Sawtry, St Neots (2), Cottenham, Sutton, Ely, Cambridge (TL) and Huntingdon (ICU and OSU).

16th April 1997 – Snailwell. Appliances were called to the premises of Mayer Parry at 04.58 hours to an incident involving 70 tonnes of scrap metal, a dust plant and a 70 m long shredder. Crews from Soham (2), Newmarket (Suffolk) (2) and Burwell plus Newmarket (Suffolk WrC), St Neots (HSRU) and Huntingdon (ICU) attended and used ten BA, six jets and a water shuttle relay.

9th February 1999 – Bottisham. Fire crews were alerted shortly after 03.00 hours to a massive fire involving the Sports Hall at the Village College. The initial attendance was from Swaffham Bulbeck and Cambridge. A subsequent '*make pumps 8*' message brought on additional pumps from Cambridge, Burwell, Sawston, Cottenham, Soham, Newmarket (2) (Suffolk) plus the TL (Cambridge), ICU and WFoU (Huntingdon) and WrC (Yaxley). The stop message at 06.11 hours stated '*Fire in a sports hall spreading through roof of swimming pool, 10 BA, 3 jets, 2 hosereels, TL monitor, 2 hydrants and water relay*'.

20th February 1999 – Horseheath. During the afternoon, crews were summoned from Linton and Haverhill (Suffolk) when a fire was reported in a commercial building. A '*make pumps 8*' message brought the second pump from Haverhill, Saffron Walden (Essex), Sawston, Cambridge, Swaffham Bulbeck and Burwell and the ICU, OSU and WFoU all from Huntingdon. The stop message, '*Fire in a single storey industrial workshop, 6 BA, 4 jets, 2 hosereels, ground monitor and water shuttle relay*' was timed at 17.26 hours.

23rd March 1999 – Sutton. A fire in a factory just before midnight caused severe damage to the roof of a warehouse some 330 feet by 200 feet. The initial attendance of pumps from Sutton and Ely immediately called for assistance and further pumps from Chatteris, Ely, Cottenham, St Ives and Soham plus the TL from Cambridge and support vehicles from Huntingdon were mobilised. The stop message timed at 01.58 hours was '*Fire in factory, 8 BA, 2 jets, 1 hosereel, 2 ground monitors, water tower and water shuttle relay*'.

24th March 1999 – Fengate, Peterborough. In the early hours crews from Dogsthorpe and Stanground responded to a severe fire in a warehouse adjacent to Peterborough Greyhound Stadium. The fire soon spread to the roof of the stadium and make-ups brought on pumps from the PVFB (2), Thorney, Whittlesey, Yaxley, Sawtry, March, Ramsey and three pumps from Lincolnshire (Crowland, Stamford and Market Deeping). Yaxley's WrC, Dogsthorpe (TL), Huntingdon (ICCU and OSU) and St Neots (HSRU) also attended. The stop was for a *'fire in a warehouse, 15 metres by 30 metres, spread to Greyhound Stadium, 100 metres by 20 metres, 10 jets, 1 TL monitor supplied by a water relay from 4 hydrants'*.

7th May 1999 – Car breakers yard, Chesterton, Cambridge. Over forty firefighters were called to deal with a fire, which broke out in a mobile car crusher and spread to hundreds of scrap cars. Eight pumps, a Water Carrier and two support appliances dealt with the fire which engulfed hundreds of cars on the site and also a ton of used tyres. The fire took 3½ hours to bring under control and the thick smoke from it caused traffic chaos to the nearby A10 and A14 trunk roads.

21st August 2000 – A1 Thornhaugh. A fatal road crash occurred on the northbound carriageway of the A1, north of the A47 junction near Wansford. The crash involved two articulated lorries and a coach carrying a group of air cadets returning to nearby RAF Wittering. There were numerous injured casualties and three of the cadets lost their lives due to the accident. Firefighters worked for several hours to release trapped cadets and to provide first aid to the injured. Over twenty casualties were taken to hospital by a fleet of ambulances.

6th September 2000 – Zion Baptist Church, East Road, Cambridge. A total of eight pumps plus 'specials' were mobilised to a fire in a church just around the corner from Cambridge Fire Station.

27th September 2000 – A14 Huntingdon. Three fire crews dealt with a road traffic accident on the A14 slip road at the Spittals Interchange, near Huntingdon, after a lorry carrying over 300 pigs overturned. Firefighters worked closely with veterinary surgeons and the RSPCA to rescue 250 of the pigs from the wreckage. They created an impromptu pen, for the rescued pigs, between the emergency vehicles and roadside crash barriers. The road was closed for four hours while the scene was made safe.

9th December 2000 – Fengate, Peterborough. Tee-Kay Packaging was the scene of a severe blaze in a single storey commercial building. Over 100 firefighters from Cambridgeshire, Lincolnshire and Northamptonshire took nearly three hours to extinguish the blaze using sixteen pumping appliances plus support vehicles including two Water Carriers.

21st March 2000 – Fowlmere. Eight fire crews and five other specialist fire service crews were called to deal with a fire at Welding Alloys Ltd, Fowlmere. The fire broke out in a large articulated skip containing one and a half tonnes of

Zion Baptist Church, Cambridge (photo – Geoff Heathcock)

chemicals including sulphur and magnesium powder. Fire crews wore breathing apparatus and chemical protection suits to tackle the blaze. The gas cloud from the fire travelled a distance of up to ten miles in one direction and members of the public in the affected areas were advised to remain indoors and to close all doors and windows. The gas cloud dissipated several hours later. The fire crews remained at the scene for more than fifteen hours to supervise the controlled burning of the residue in the skip.

31st July 2000 – Bar Hill. Over fifty firefighters dealt with a chemical incident on a busy industrial estate after a chemical reaction occurred in the back of a refuse lorry. Hundreds of workers had to be evacuated from local factories during the operation, which lasted over five hours. Once the Fire and Rescue Service had brought the incident under control a convoy of emergency vehicles took the contained chemicals to a waste disposal site. There were no injuries to either firefighters or local workers.

13th December 2000 – M11 Motorway, Girton. Over twenty firefighters spent more than three hours tackling a blaze in an articulated lorry containing diesel fuel and plastic buckets. The retained crew from Cottenham were first to arrive on the scene and found the lorry well alight and all lanes of the motorway had to be closed as thick black smoke was drifting across the carriageways.

Firefighters had to be extremely cautious of the number of cylinders involved as they periodically exploded during the incident.

6th March 2001 – Fengate, Peterborough. Just after 20.00 hours over 100 firefighters converged on a huge fire at the headquarters of the Ideal World Shopping Network on Newark Road. Sixteen fire appliances and several other specialist support appliances, including both of the Service's Turntable Ladders were required to deal with the fire which broke out while the network was live on television, with over 150 staff in the building. Although no-one was injured during the evacuation it was initially thought that one person had been left behind in the building. Fire crews in breathing apparatus entered the building to carry out a search but the missing person was found outside, safe and well. Two firefighters suffered slightly from smoke inhalation and were given oxygen treatment at the scene. In less than two hours the rapidly escalating blaze had destroyed the 72,500 sq. ft. building causing structural damage to 75 per cent of the premises. Local residents were forced to close their windows as thick black smoke drifted over a large area of Peterborough; Newark Road itself was closed for five days due to the dense smoke still issuing from the building. The fire was under control by 22.20 hours but fire crews stayed at the scene for a week tackling small fires in the wreckage of the building. Water Tender Ladders attended from Dogsthorpe, Stanground, PVFB (2), Thorney, Whittlesey, Yaxley, Sawtry, Ramsey (2), March, Chatteris, Oundle (Northants) and Crowland, Market Deeping and Stamford (all from Lincs.). Turntable Ladders

Ideal World Shopping Network TV Studios, Peterborough (photo – *Peterborough Evening Telegraph*)

from Dogsthorpe and Cambridge, the Incident Control Unit and Incident Support Unit both from Huntingdon completed the attendance.

10th March 2001 – Linton. It took firefighters over two hours to rescue a female who was walking on a path, which collapsed. She fell some 20 feet below ground level into an ancient well. The hole was 8 feet wide and firefighters at the scene needed to use a Turntable Ladder as an anchor point from which they could be lowered by winch to carry out the rescue. Doctors at the scene liaised with firefighters, who were working in the well during the rescue, to ensure that it was safe to lift the trapped lady from her predicament

4th September 2001 – Offord Cluny. Over seventy firefighters from Cambridgeshire and Bedfordshire with seventeen fire appliances, including the Turntable Ladders from Cambridge and Peterborough, attended a serious fire at RWH Enterprises, Station Lane, Offord Cluny. Firefighters used twelve jets to fight the fire from outside the 150 metres by 50 metres factory premises. The Turntable Ladders were also used as water towers. It took firefighters 4½ hours, using water pumped from the nearby River Ouse, to bring the fire under control and operations continued at the scene for a number of days. The extent of the damage to the building was so severe that the cause of the fire was never established.

22nd November 2001 – Peterborough Cathedral. Potentially one of the most serious fires to occur in Peterborough was averted by the quick thinking of Cathedral staff and the quick response of fire crews from the city, when Fire Control began receiving calls at 18.40 hours. The PDA of pumps from Dogsthorpe and Stanground together with the TL and RV from Dogsthorpe were immediately mobilised. Due to the number of calls being received, control ordered on an additional pump from the PVFB. Crews entering the building located the fire very quickly using thermal imaging cameras in the thick smoke. An immediate 'Make pumps 5' message brought on Yaxley and Whittlesey. The

RWH Enterprises, Offord Cluny (photo – *Hunts. Post*)

The scene outside Peterborough Cathedral (photo – Author's collection)

Inside Peterborough Cathedral the next day (photo – *Peterborough Evening Telegraph*)

Rescue Damage Control Unit from Cambridge was also sent on to assist with salvage work. Further make-ups brought on a total of eleven appliances manned by fifty firefighters. The stop message was timed at 20.29 hours and 15 BA, one jet and a number of hosereels were in use. Damage to the historic Cathedral was minimised and restricted to some stacks of plastic chairs, one of the buildings leaded windows and wooden casing at the rear of the church organ which was also charred and burned. There was no structural damage to the Cathedral, although the historic painted ceiling did sustain some smoke damage. The organ itself was out of action for many months while it was being cleaned and restored.

7th May 2002 – Magdalene College, Cambridge. A call to a potentially serious incident was received at 16.40 hours to a fire in an accommodation block of the college in the heart of the city. Six pumps from Cambridge (2), Cottenham, Swaffham Bulbeck, Burwell and Papworth Everard plus the RV and TL from Cambridge attended. The stop message was received at 17.19 hours with '*4 BA, 1 jet and 1 hosereel in use*'.

28th June 2002 – Clayhithe. Shortly before 03.00 hours one pump from each of Cottenham and Cambridge fire stations were sent to *The Bridge Hotel*. On arrival, a large outhouse was found to well alight with fire spreading to the kitchen. The hotel was heavily smoke-logged with the asbestos roof of the outhouse involved. A '*make pumps 6*' message was sent which brought on the second pump from Cambridge plus Swaffham Bulbeck, Burwell and Ely, together with the ICU from Huntingdon. The stop message stating '*12 BA, 2 jets and 4 hosereels*' was sent at 04.35 hours.

28th December 2002 – Wisbech. One appliance from Wisbech was sent to a rubbish fire close to a food packaging warehouse in the town. The fire involved a large pile of rubbish containing five gas cylinders, which rapidly spread to involve the inside of the building and then penetrated a second attached warehouse. Further pumps attended from Wisbech, March, Thorney, Whittlesey, Chatteris and Ramsey. Dogsthorpe (TL), Huntingdon (ICU, RV and OSU) completed the attendance from Cambridgeshire. Norfolk sent pumps from Outwell, West Walton, Terrington, Downham Market and Kings Lynn. Long Sutton (Lincolnshire) completed the attendance.

13th January 2003 – Yelling. A smoke alarm no doubt saved the lives of three people when their large detached thatched cottage was destroyed by fire. Fire broke out on the first floor of the property at about 04.00 hours, when all the occupants, a couple and their nine-year-old son, were asleep. Crews from Papworth Everard, St Neots and Huntingdon were sent on the initial attendance. As a consequence of make up messages, additional pumps from St Neots, Huntingdon, Gamlingay, St Ives (2), Cambridge (2) and Sawtry attended. The ICU and OSU (Huntingdon) and the WrC from Kempston in Bedfordshire were also in attendance. The stop message was '*detached thatched property with* *summer room, 20 metres by 10 metres, 100% well alight, 8 BA, 5 jets, 2 hydrants and open water. Two casualties taken to hospital with minor burns and smoke inhalation'*.

15th January 2003 – *Regent Hotel*, Cambridge. A call was received at 17.40 hours to a fire in the basement of the *Regent Hotel*, Cambridge. A Chinese restaurant occupied the basement and the crews were faced with a rapidly developing fire, which was accessing the ventilation ducts. A *'make pumps 5, turntable ladder required'* message was sent followed by further make-ups finally reaching *'make pumps 20, turntable ladders 2'*. The hotel was evacuated without any injuries and the fire spread to the upper floors and roof causing severe damage. Pumps attended from Cambridge (2), Swaffham Bulbeck, Cottenham, Sawston, Papworth, St Ives (2), Burwell, Ely (2), Sutton, St Neots (2), Gamlingay, Soham, Linton, Ramsey, Newmarket (Suffolk), Bury St Edmunds (Suffolk) and Royston (Hertfordshire). Two TLs from Dogsthorpe and Bury St Edmunds (Suffolk) plus the ICU and OSU from Huntingdon were also in attendance.

23rd February 2003 – Cambridge Science Park, Cambridge. At 08.30 hours the Fire Service, Ambulance and Police were called to a sulphurous smell at the Cambridge Science Park where twenty-eight people had been affected by dizziness and runny noses. By lunchtime the cause had been traced to a build up of hydrogen sulphide. Appliances attending were from Cambridge (2), Sawston, Cottenham, Burwell, St Neots and St Ives supported by the Huntingdon Incident Control Unit, St Neots Hazardous Substances Rescue Unit and the Yaxley Water Carrier.

3rd March 2003 – near Manea. This early evening call brought on appliances from Manea and Chatteris plus the RV from Huntingdon to the scene of a microlight aircraft which had crashed next to the March to Ely railway line. It took crews some two hours to release the pilot, the only person on board.

14th March 2003 – Gamlingay. The initial call was to a *'chimney fire in a thatched property'* and Gamlingay, supported by Potton (WrT and L4P) from Bedfordshire were mobilised. On arrival the thatched roof was found to be well alight and a *'make pumps 4, water carrier required'* message was sent. St Neots, Papworth Everard and the water carrier from Kempston (Bedfordshire) completed this make-up. A *'make pumps 6'* message brought on two pumps from Royston (Hertfordshire). The RV, ICU and OSU all from Huntingdon completed the attendance along with the OSU from Bedford, sent to support BA wearers from Bedfordshire, and eight BA, one jet and two hosereels were used to extinguish the fire.

29th July 2003 – Godmanchester. At 20.22 hours, two pumps from Huntingdon were mobilised to a transformer and electrical substation fire. The substation was situated adjacent to the A14 road flyover, which had to be closed during the incident. On arrival the substation was well alight and the 33,000 volt transformer was becoming heavily involved and even with the electricity isolated the connections required earthing to reduce residual voltage problems. Further pumps attending were St Ives (2), Ramsey, Sawtry and St Neots with the HSRU (St Neots), RV, ICU and W/FoU all from Huntingdon making up the final attendance. Six covering jets and two foam jets (AFFF) were used to extinguish the fire and although the stop message was sent at 23.56 hours the incident continued for several days with a combined fire fighting and environmental role.

2nd October 2003 – Kitchen Range Foods, Huntingdon. One pump from Huntingdon was mobilised at 21.37 hours to an AFA at this address. On arrival the crew found a fire involving an industrial fryer unit and extraction system. Further crews were requested and in total eight pumps from Huntingdon (2), St Ives (2), Sawtry, Ramsey, St Neots and Papworth Everard attended. The ICU and OSU from Huntingdon were also in attendance. Six BA, two hosereels and cutting equipment were used to extinguish the fire.

22nd December 2003 – Great North Road, Eaton Socon. Two pumps from St Neots were mobilised at 16.40 hours to a fire in a factory unit. By 17.32 hours the incident had grown to '*make pumps 12, turntable ladder required*'. Crews from Gamlingay, Kimbolton, Huntingdon (2) plus ICU and OSU, Papworth Everard, Sawtry, St Ives (2) with 2 pumps from Bedfordshire (Sandy and Potton) made up the attendance. The stop message at 18.46 hours stated '*fire in factory, 30 metres by 30 metres, used for battery charging, 5 jets, 1 hosereel, TL monitor, 4 hydrants in use*'.

12th February 2004 – Whittlesey. There was an explosion and fire at Anvil Engineering, Whittlesey. Pumps from Whittlesey and Stanground made up the initial attendance which quickly grew to include Thorney, Dogsthorpe, PVFB (2), Ramsey, Yaxley, Chatteris and Crowland (Lincolnshire). Cambridge (TL), Huntingdon (ICU and OSU) and the Red Cross FVSU from Whittlesey also attended. This very testing incident involved industrial premises 100 metres by 50 metres. Four BA and three jets were used and crews recovered the bodies of two deceased workers.

7th March 2004 – Scrap yard, March. Pumps from March (2) and Chatteris were sent to the Fen Breakers scrap yard, March at 13.44 hours after a number of repeat calls. Following make-up messages, pumps from Wisbech (2), Whittlesey, Thorney, Yaxley, Manea also attended plus Dogsthorpe (TL), Huntingdon (ICU and WFoU). In total over 100 cars were involved in the fire with six BA, eight jets and water from both hydrants and open water being used.

27th March 2004 – Elton Hall, Elton. At 17.03 hours a call was received at Fire Control to a fire at Elton Hall, Elton. The fire in the basement of this

Anvil Engineering, Whittlesey (photo – Tony Lovelock)

historic building was attended by ten pumps from Yaxley, Stanground, Dogs-thorpe, PVFB, Sawtry, Whittlesey, Thorney, Oundle (Northants), Stamford (Lincs.) and Crowland (Lincs.). The Turntable Ladder (Dogsthorpe), Water Carrier (Yaxley), Incident Control and the Ops Support Units (both from Huntingdon) also attended this incident.

18th April 2004 – Abbotsley. Two pumps from St Neots were mobilised at 05:32 hours to the High Street, Abbotsley where there was a report of a fire in a thatched cottage. Due to Fire Control receiving many calls to this incident an additional pump from Gamlingay was also sent. En-route to the incident the OIC of the first crew could see that the roof of the 12 metres by 6 metres building was heavily involved in fire and immediately sent a message '*make pumps 5*'. On receipt of this message control sent on Papworth and one pump from Huntingdon, along with the OSU and ICU both also from Huntingdon. To assist with salvage work a further make up message was sent and Kimbolton, Huntingdon (2nd pump) and St Ives (2 pumps) were mobilised. Twelve BA, two jets, two hosereels and an open water supply were used to extinguish the blaze.

21st June 2004 – Fenstanton. At 18.14 hours pumps from St Ives and Papworth and the HSRU from St Neots were sent to the Dairycrest Dairy, High Street where a fire in the plant room had caused an ammonia leak. Subsequently pumps from St Neots, Huntingdon (2), Cottenham, Cambridge

Fire in thatched cottage, Abbotsley (photo – Geoff Heathcock)

and Ramsey attended plus the RV, WrFC and ICU (all Huntingdon) and the OSU (March). Six BA, four gas tight suits, two hosereels and decontamination were used to deal with the leak. The stop message was sent at 23.33 hours.

2nd August 2004 – Peterborough. At 10.56 hours pumps from the PVFB and Yaxley were mobilised to a fire in Abdullah's fast food shop, Long Causeway. The incident progressed to '*make pumps 6, turntable ladder required*' with supporting appliances attending from Dogsthorpe, Stanground, Thorney, and Sawtry. These pumps were supplemented by the Turntable Ladder from Dogsthorpe and the Ops Support Unit from March. The stop message was timed at 12.34 hours '*Fire in roof space of 3 storey commercial building, 6 BA, 1 jet, TL monitor, and 2 hydrants*'.

Saturday, 30th October 2004 – Morborne. A 580-feet-high Transmitter Mast collapsed after a serious fire. National and local radio channels to 1.3 million homes over large areas of Cambridgeshire, Bedfordshire, Buckinghamshire, Leicestershire, Lincolnshire, Norfolk and Northamptonshire were out of action for many days. Mobile phone users were also affected. Crews from Yaxley, Dogsthorpe, Stanground and PVFB attended.

27th October 2004 – Mayfield Primary School, Histon Road, Cambridge. At 20.20 hours two pumps from Cambridge responded to a fire at this school. On arrival these crews were faced with a severe and rapidly developing fire and immediate assistance was requested and further crews from Cottenham,

Swaffham Bulbeck, Burwell, Papworth, St Ives (2), Linton, Ely, Sawston, Sutton, Gamlingay, Newmarket (Suffolk) and Royston (Hertfordshire) attended. Special appliances attending were Cambridge (TL), Huntingdon (ICU) and March (OSU). In total over 100 firefighters attended and took seven hours to extinguish the fire, which affected six classrooms, toilets and changing rooms. Extensive water damage was caused to the kitchens and the main hall. Other rooms were damaged by smoke.

21st April 2005 – Kelly Vision, Peterborough Road, Whittlesey. The Fire & Rescue Service was called to this address twice in the same evening. The first call was received by fire control at 17.56 hours and pumps from Whittlesey and Stanground were mobilised to these commercial premises of two floors and a basement. Following a succession of make-ups, additional pumps from Thorney, PVFB, Yaxley and Ramsey (2) were in attendance plus the TL from Dogsthorpe, ICU from Huntingdon and OSU from March. Three jets, three hosereels and twenty BA were used to extinguish the blaze. Later the same evening, at 23.36 hours another call was received to the same address and again Whittlesey and Stanground were mobilised. Thorney, Dogsthorpe and the TL from Dogsthorpe attended as make-up crews and this time one TL monitor, three hosereels and twelve BA were in use to control the outbreak.

1st July 2005 – Bar Hill. Two pumps from Cambridge Fire Station were mobilised to a fire in a warehouse in Trafalgar Way. Subsequent make-ups brought on pumps from Sawston, St Ives (2), Huntingdon, Ely and Royston (Herts.). The TL from Cambridge, the RV and ICU from Huntingdon and the

'The incident control point' at Whittlesey April 2005, (left) Ops Support Unit and (centre) Incident Command Unit (photo – Geoff Heathcock)

OSU from March were also in attendance. The stop was timed at 14.35 hours and stated that it was a fire in a warehouse, three other premises were also affected, total area 80 metres by 25 metres and four hosereels were used to extinguish the fire.

3rd October 2005 – Castle Camps. At 20.47 hours a call was received to a fire in a thatched roof at Elizabeth Cottage in the High Street. The Linton crew plus two crews from Haverhill (Suffolk) were mobilised and the first pump was in attendance at 21.01 hours and immediately sent a make-up message '*make pumps 6*'. Additional pumps from Cambridge, Sawston and two from Saffron Walden (Essex) were sent on plus the Incident Command Unit (Huntingdon) and the Ops Support Unit (March). The first informative message at 21.14 hours advised that '*a thatched cottage roof void was well alight, 2 BA, 2 hosereels in use, salvage work in progress*'. At 21.42 hours a water carrier was requested and at 21.55 hours a '*make pumps 10*' message was sent. Yaxley and Newmarket (Suffolk) Water Carriers were mobilised along with pumps from Cambridge (2nd), Swaffham Bulbeck, Burwell and Clare (Suffolk). The stop message was sent at 04.01 hours as follows '*2 storey thatched cottage, approx. 25 metres by 8 metres, 6 BA, 4 jets, 4 hosereels, hydrants and water carriers in use*'.

10th February 2006 – Sibson Airfield. A call was received in Fire Control at 04.53 to a building on fire at this airfield which is used for light aircraft and as a parachuting centre. Pumps from Stanground and Yaxley were immediately mobilised. Whilst still en-route to the incident the OIC of the Stanground appliance requested the attendance of a water carrier and then on arrival sent a make up message '*make pumps 6*'. Following these requests, pumps from Dogsthorpe, PVFB, Oundle (Northants) and Stamford (2) (Lincs.) were sent on plus the Water Foam Unit from Huntingdon. The Hazardous Materials Unit from St Neots was sent as control unit due to the unavailability of the Incident Command Unit and the Ops Support Unit (March) completed the attendance. The stop message was sent at 08.18 hours detailing '*fire in single storey building 20 metres by 7 metres used as Birdland Bar, additional single storey building 6 metres by 5 metres used for storage and beer cellar type building 4 metres by 3 metres, 4 BA, 3 jets, water shuttle from hydrant*'.

PART SIX

PETERBOROUGH VOLUNTEER
FIRE BRIGADE

Chapter 15

PETERBOROUGH VOLUNTEER FIRE BRIGADE

I N 1872 an attempt was made at forming a Volun-teer Fire Brigade by a group of local businessmen and tradesmen, but it was not until after the disastrous Infirmary Fire of 1884 that the Peter-borough Volunteer Fire Brigade (PVFB) finally came into being. The first equipment used by the PVFB; hose, hosereel, standpipes etc., were kept in the coach house of the *Angel Hotel*. The first Captain of the new brigade was John Vergette, a draper by trade, and in 1891 Fireman John Brooks allowed a timber shed to be built in his baker's yard to become the first true Fire Station.

Badge of the Peterborough Volunteer Fire Brigade

Brigade members with Hose Cart outside Brooks Yard Fire Station (photo – Peterborough Volunteer Fire Brigade)

By 1894 the brigade was the proud owner of two vehicles; a Hose Truck for carrying many items of loose equipment and a Shand Mason Curricle Fire Escape, however it was not until 1908 that the brigade acquired a steam powered fire engine, again manufactured by Shand Mason.

In 1903 electric call bells, connected to the Fire Station, were fitted in the homes and business premises of members of the brigade. Prior to this they relied on call boys to bring them into the station. Up until 1927 the senior officer of the brigade was known as Captain and his subordinate officer as Lieutenant, but in 1928 it appears that the rank names were changed to Chief Officer and Second Officer. Meanwhile a new post had been created in 1908 when the brigade's steam fire engine was purchased, that of Engineer, whose skills were required to maintain and operate the engine.

When John Brooks retired from business in 1919 the new owners of his shop continued to allow the brigade to use the fire station in their yard but it became apparent that it was rapidly becoming too small and the brigade were actively looking for a site to buy and build a new fire station. Eventually a plot was found in King Street, containing 126½ sq.yds., and this was purchased in 1922. The new station of a single storey brick design was opened in November of that year.

Peterborough Volunteer Fire Brigade with equipment in the early 1900s
(photo – Peterborough Volunteer Fire Brigade)

The first King Street Fire Station (photo – Peterborough Volunteer Fire Brigade)

It was about 15 feet wide and about 41 feet long although the committee room at the rear reduced the depth by some 8 feet. At this time, fire calls were received by the City Fire Brigade at their station in Queen Street, just around the corner, where Fireman Long and his wife lived. It was their responsibility to ring the call bells to alert both the City Brigade and the PVFB and one of the responding members of the PVFB would then have to call in the Queen Street station to collect a message giving the location of the fire.

In 1913 the brigade had become motorised when they purchased an Argyll Motor Tender built to carry eight men plus equipment and able to tow the steamer. This was replaced in 1923 with a Model 'T' Ford tender and towing vehicle and 1925 saw the purchase of a motor trailer pump. The brigade had been entering into agreements with Local Authorities, outside of Peterborough, to provide fire cover and now being motorised it allowed them to go much further distances. By 1925 the brigade had agreements from as far away as Baston (Lincolnshire), Lutton (Northamptonshire), Sawtry (Huntingdonshire) and Whittlesey (Isle of Ely) giving an average radius of around 15 miles from Peterborough. At this time the City Fire Brigade only attended fires within the city boundaries unless specifically authorised by the mayor. In the city area itself both the PVFB and the City Brigade worked alongside each other, with fire calls being relayed to both stations, sometimes with a certain amount of animosity, probably due to the fact that most of the members of the City Brigade were waterworks employees and also lived all over the city. This meant that it took them longer to reach their station than the volunteers who nearly all lived in

1923 Model T Ford Tender and Towing Vehicle (photo – Peterborough Volunteer Fire Brigade)

1925 Dennis Trailer Pump (photo – Peterborough Volunteer Fire Brigade)

their city centre business premises and consequently they frequently got to fires before the City Brigade.

Finally in 1930 the Brigade became the proud owners of its first self-propelled motor fire engine; a 45 hp Dennis appliance with a pumping capacity of 350 gpm and carried a 30 feet Ajax ladder all of which greatly and rapidly enhanced the Brigade's capabilities.

1930 Dennis Pump FL8570 (photo – George Dunlop collection)

The year 1934 saw the purchase of the Brigade's first enclosed fire appliance; a Bedford van which could be used as a towing vehicle. Along with all the other fire appliances this had been purchased with the monies earned at fires and by public subscription.

In 1941, along with rest of the country, the PVFB was absorbed into the National Fire Service, although it did manage to retain much of its own special background. The brigade was divided into three sections, each under the control of a senior member. These sections took it in turn to sleep on the station each night to ensure a rapid turn-out. The second section would be called in on a 'yellow alert' and the third section came in when the sirens sounded. Apart from the air-raids on Spalding in 1941 and Peterborough itself in 1942 the most eventual time came in 1942 when two contingents of the brigade visited London on separate occasions as relief crews for the London Fire Brigade.

In 1942 the NFS took away the Bedford Tender and replaced it with an Austin ATV and trailer pump combination, which was itself replaced by a similar vehicle in 1947.

When the 1947 Fire Services Act returned control to local authorities, the initial proposals indicated that there was no place in the modern service for a volunteer brigade. However, following a number of meetings with the new Soke of Peterborough County Council and its Chief Fire Officer designate, a role was found for the PVFB. This was no doubt due to the fact that the Soke of

Peterborough Volunteer Fire Brigade 1942 (photo – Peterborough Volunteer Fire Brigade)

Peterborough was one of smallest county authorities in the country and therefore could make good use of the resources of the PVFB. An agreement was signed by both parties and this has been upheld by the different county councils created by the subsequent local government re-organisations.

The first appliance received by the brigade post-war in 1949 was another ATV which had been converted into a Hosereel Tender towing a trailer pump.

Following the great fire at Robert Sayle in 1956, reported on elsewhere in this book, the Fire Station in King Street was repaired and later in that year the old pre-war Dennis Pump was replaced with a Dennis F8 Pump Escape, ex-Dogsthorpe. Subsequent redevelopment of the Robert Sayle store brought the need for further change. The existing station was very narrow and it became desirable to build a larger two bay station.

Discussions were held with the Co-Operative Permanent Building Society to build a single storey station with two floors above for commercial use.

On the 19th July 1960 the brigade vacated its station and moved into temporary premises at the Westgate Motor Company's Garage in Queen Street, but it was not until June 1962 that the new station was completed and the brigade finally moved in. The last of the 'old' type appliances, the Austin Hosereel Tender, was replaced in 1962 by a 1950 Dennis F12 Pump Escape, handed down from Dogsthorpe Fire Station and converted to carry a 30 ft extension ladder. Since then the appliance fleet has regularly been kept up to date by the various local authority fire services.

The opening of the new station was overshadowed by the announcement of outline plans for extensive housing estates and a massive re-development of the City Centre. However, it was not until 1967 that the official announcements were made and the City Centre development, which affected the station most, did not commence until nearly 10 years later. The major project was the large Queensgate shopping complex, which was built across King Street, severing northern access to Westgate. Although early intentions were to stay on the same site, with some alterations, eventually an alternative site was found in Bourges Boulevard. Negotiations were entered into to sell the King Street site and to purchase the new site. Once this was completed plans were drawn up and building commenced. The station was completed in less than a year and was officially opened by HRH The Duke of Gloucester on the 17th August 1982.

On the 28th July 1984 the PVFB celebrated its centenary and in a mark of appreciation by the City Council the brigade was granted the freedom of the City of Peterborough. This event was unique in two ways, firstly the brigade is the only Volunteer Fire Brigade to have reached 100 years of service and secondly the only Fire Brigade in the UK to be granted the freedom of a city.

The PVFB has always been held in great esteem by the local community and has always worked in an excellent co-operative manner with local industry. Proof of this was shown in 1992 when the Baker Perkins Works Fire Brigade was disbanded and their Land Rover fire appliance was donated to the PVFB

The new King Street Fire Station (photo – Peterborough Volunteer Fire Brigade)

Crest on outside wall of Bourges Boulevard Fire Station (photo – Pete Ashpool collection)

After the Centenary Parade, Peterborough (photo – Peterborough Volunteer Fire Brigade)

Presentation of the Freedom of the City Certificate (photo – Peterborough Volunteer Fire Brigade)

1963 'M' Series Land Rover L4P REG 999 (photo – Peterborough Volunteer Fire Brigade)

Dennis Rolls Water Tender Ladder YEG 729J (photo – David Palmer)

and is now held in a preserved role. Another fire appliance which is held in a preserved role is the Dennis Rolls Water Tender Ladder YEG 729J, which was delivered new to the PVFB in 1971.

Chief Officers of the Brigade

Name	Occupation	Dates
John Vergette	Draper	1884–1890
Joseph Clifton	Publican	1890–1892
Henry Clarabut	Draper	1892–1905
John Brooks	Baker	1905–1924
George Dickens	Monumental mason	1924–1928
John Johnson	Butcher	1928–1936
William Blackman	Tobacconist	1936–1946
Stanley Cooke	Music shop owner	1946–1950
Thomas Dickens	Monumental mason	1950–1961
Frederick Johnson, B.E.M.	Butcher	1961–1965
Hubert Willis	Electrical contractor	1965–1970
Derrick Shrive	Chemist	1970–1975
Alan Morton	Printer	1975–1980
John Thompson	Furniture maker	1980–1985
Geoff Sayers, M.B.E., M.I.Fire E.	Chartered builder	1985–2000
Russell Evans	Postman	2000–2002
Antonio De Matteis	Prison officer	2003–

Note: Blank spaces indicate that details are unable to be confirmed.

Water Tenders – special notes

'War-time'   A converted lorry with either a canvas dam with a steel frame or a galvanised iron tank fitted to the lorry bed. A hosereel was fitted together with a light pump. The unit invariably towed a trailer pump.

'Type A'   A post-war development of the above, carrying 400 gallons of water, 2×180 ft. hosereels and carrying a light detachable pump. A trailer pump was also towed.

'Type B'   As above but fitted with a main pump driven via the road engine
(from 1955) and carrying a light portable pump. Could run as either a Water Tender or a Water Tender Ladder depending on the type of ladder carried.

(*Continued*)

PRE-WAR FIRE APPLIANCES

Reg.	Type	Date	Manufacturer	Details	Sold
	Hose Tender	1913	Argyll	PVFB	1920
	Towing Vehicle for steamer	1920	Austin	PVFB	1923
CE 7352	Pump	1921	Dennis N	Cambridge Borough Police	
	Towing Vehicle	1923	Ford Model T	PVFB	1934
FL 3232	Pump	1923	Ford Model T	Peterborough City	
	Pump	1927	Dennis G	Ely	
	Pump	1927	Dennis G	Old Fletton	
	Pump	1927	Dennis G	Chatteris	
	Pump	1929	Dennis	St Ives	
FL 8570	Pump	1930	Dennis	PVFB	1956
EW 6681	Pump	1930	Dennis	Borough of Huntingdon	
	Pump	1931	Dennis	Peterborough City	1950
EB 9734	Pump Escape	1932	Leyland FT1	Borough of Wisbech	
EG 1074	Towing Vehicle for trailer pump	1934	Bedford	PVFB	Preserved 1942 **(1)**
EW 8489	Pump	1934	Dennis Ace	St Neots U.D.C.	1958
DER 640	Pump	1934	Dennis Ace Limousine	Fordham	1963 **(2)**
JE 1064	Pump	1934	Leyland Cub FK4	March U.D.C.	
AER 2	TL	1934	Albion/Merryweather	Cambridge Borough Police	1953
EW 9795	Pump	1936	Leyland FT6	Yaxley Parish	
JE 4222	Pump	1938	Leyland FK6	Borough of Wisbech, Thorney	
DVE 600	Pump	1938	Leyland FK8A	Cambridge Borough	

(1) Taken into NFS stock 1942.
(2) Converted post-war to Emergency Salvage Tender at Cambridge.

NFS FIRE APPLIANCES

Reg.	Type	Date	Manufacturer	Details	Sold
GGX 535	ATV/Trailer Pump	1942	Austin K2	Ely	
GLE 583	ATV/Trailer Pump	1942	Austin K2	PVFB	1947
GLR 437	ATV/Trailer Pump	1942	Austin K2	Gamlingay	(3)
GLR 796	ATV/Trailer Pump	1942	Austin K2	Linton	
GXA 792	Escape Carrying Unit	1942	Austin K4	Ely	
GXA 100	TL	1943	Dennis Merryweather	Cambridge	1948
GXH 483	ATV/Trailer Pump	1943	Austin K2	Cottenham	(3)
GXH 709	ATV/Trailer Pump	1943	Austin K2	Soham	(3)
GXH 710	ATV/Trailer Pump	1943	Austin K2	Cambridge	
	Heavy Unit	1944	Fordson 7V/Sulzer pump	Dogsthorpe	1957
GLW 436	TL	1943	Dennis Lancet/Merryweather	Dogsthorpe	1965
GXO 483	Major Dam Unit	1944	Dodge 82A/Tangye pump	Dogsthorpe	1956
GGX 482	ATV/Trailer Pump	1947	Austin K2	PVFB	1949

(3) Converted to carry ladders within bodywork to fit into low station.

CAMBRIDGESHIRE FIRE APPLIANCES 1948–1965

Reg.	Type	Date	Manufacturer	Details	Sold
HVE 699	WrC	1950 (ex RAF)	Dodge	Cambridge	1956
	Wrt	1951	Bedford QL	Gamlingay	1953
JVE 222	PE	1952	Dennis F12	Cambridge	1972
KCE 820	P	1953	Dennis F8	Soham	1972
LCE 212	TL	1953	Dennis F14/Metz	Cambridge	1979
LER 999	PL	1953	Dennis F8	Cambridge	
LVE 562	WrT	1953	Bedford SB/Wilsdon	Gamlingay, Manea	1978
NER 20	WrT	1954	Bedford SB/Wilsdon	Swaffham Bulbeck	1975
NER 21	WrT	1954	Bedford SB/Wilsdon	Cambridge, Linton	1975
OER 27	WrT	1955	Bedford SB/Wilsdon	Cambridge/Manea	
OVE 400	WrT	1955	Bedford RLHZ/Haydon	Soham, Whittlesford	1971

Reg.	Date	Manufacturer	Type	Details	Sold
PCE 829	1956	Bedford RLHZ 4×4/Marshall/Sun	WrC	Cambridge, Wisbech, Whittlesey	1977
PVE 422	1956	Bedford RLHZ 4×4/Haydon	WrT	Cottenham	
SCE 118	1957	Bedford RLHZ 4×4/Haydon	WrT	Soham, Swaffham Bulbeck	1975
VER 667	1958	Bedford RLHZ 4×4/Wilsdon	WrT	Cambridge, Sawston	1979
XVE 235	1961	Bedford RLHZ 4×4/Haydon	WrT	Papworth, Burwell	1979
115 CER	1963	Bedford RLHZ 4×4/Papworth	EST	Cambridge	1979

HUNTINGDONSHIRE COUNTY FIRE APPLIANCES 1948–1965

Reg.	Date	Manufacturer	Type	Details	Sold
GLE 196	1942	Austin K2	ATV	St Neots	1963 **(4)**
GXH 472	1943	Austin K2	ATV	Huntingdon	**(4)**
KEW 952	1952	Bedford SL/Miles	PE	Huntingdon, St Neots	pre 1971
NEW 500	1954	Bedford TJ4/Miles	WrT	Huntingdon, St Ives	pre 1971
OEW 345	1955	Bedford TJ4/Miles	WrT	Yaxley	1967
PEW 789	1957	Bedford SL/Miles	WrT	Huntingdon, Ramsey	1971
SEW 329	1957	Bedford SL/Miles	WrT	Huntingdon, St Neots	1975
TEW 707	1957	Bedford TJ4/Miles	WrT	Kimbolton	
VEW 606	1959	Bedford TJ4/Miles	WrT	Sawtry	
XEW 686	1960	Bedford SL/Miles	WrT	Huntingdon	1975
680 DEW	1963	Bedford TJ4/Miles	WrT	Huntingdon, Thorney	1979
330 GEW	1963	Bedford TJ4/Miles	WrT	Huntingdon, Ramsey	1979
337 GEW	1963	Bedford TJ4/Miles	WrT	St Neots	
700 KEW	1963	Bedford TKEL/Miles	WrT	Yaxley, PVFB	1980
311 LEW	1964	Bedford TKEL/HCB Angus	EST	Huntingdon	1982

(4) Supplied post-war as a Hosereel Tender towing a trailer pump.

ISLE OF ELY FIRE APPLIANCES 1948–1965

Reg.	Date	Manufacturer	Type	Details	Sold
GYR 819	1950	Bedford QL (Ex Army lorry)	WrC	Wisbech	**(5)**
CJE 604	1952	Bedford SH/Cuerden	WrT	Littleport, Manea	1971
CJE 605	1952	Bedford SH/Cuerden	WrT	Wisbech, Whittlesey	1971

Reg.	Type	Manufacturer	Date	Details	Sold
DJE 92	WrL	Bedford SH/Cuerden	1953	Ely, March	1971
GJE 904	WrT	Bedford RLHZ 4×4/HCB	1959	Wisbech	1975
KEB 50	WrT	Bedford RLHZ/HCB	1959	Ely	
LJE 850	WrT	Bedford RLHZ 4×4/Smith	1960	Sutton	
NEB 945	WrT	Bedford RLHZ 4×4/Smith	1961	March	
OJE 634	WrT	Bedford RLHZ 4×4/Smith	1962	Ely, Chatteris	1979 (6)
OEB 939	PE/WrT	Bedford TKEL/HCB	1964	Wisbech	1983 (6)
AJE 350B	PE/WrT	Bedford TKEL/HCB	1964	Ely, St Neots	

(5) Fitted with stack grab.
(6) Later converted to Water Tender.

SOKE OF PETERBOROUGH FIRE APPLIANCES 1948–1965

Reg.	Type	Manufacturer	Date	Details	Sold
GLC 652	ATV	Austin K2	1949	PVFB	1962 (7)
AEG 303	PE/P	Dennis F12	1950	Dogsthorpe, PVFB	1967 (8)
FEG 603	PE	Dennis F8/Miles	1956	Dogsthorpe, PVFB	1970
GFL 507	WrT	Thorneycroft Nubian/Carmichael	1957	Dogsthorpe	1969
REG 492	PE	Dennis F28	1962	Dogsthorpe, PVFB	1979 (9)
BFL 785C	TL	AEC Mercury/Merryweather	1965	Dogsthorpe	1984
CFL 887C	EST	Bedford TKEL/Dennis M	1965	Dogsthorpe, Wisbech	1985

(7) Supplied post-war as a Hosereel Tender towing a trailer pump.
(8) Later converted to a Pump.
(9) Converted to a WrL and written off following an accident.

CAMBRIDGESHIRE & ISLE OF ELY FIRE APPLIANCES 1965–1974

Reg.	Type	Manufacturer	Date	Details	Sold
EJE 137D	WrT	Bedford RLHZ/HCB Angus	1965	Littleport, Whittlesey	1983
FVE 252D	WrT	Bedford RLHZ/HCB Angus	1965	Whittlesey	1984
GCE 481E	ET	Land Rover 109/Carmichael	1967	Wisbech	1982
HCE 486F	WrL	Bedford TKEL/HCB Angus	1968	Cambridge, St Ives	

Reg.	Type	Date	Manufacturer	Details	Sold
HVE 939F	WrC	1968	Bedford RLHZ/HCB Angus	Cambridge, Wisbech	1984
KVE 576G	WrL	1969	Bedford TKEL/HCB Angus	Cambridge, Soham	1985
KVE 577G	WrL	1969	Bedford TKEL/HCB Angus	Cambridge, March	1983
NCE 517H	WrT	1970	Bedford TKEL/HCB Angus	Gamlingay, Burwell	
NCE 518H	WrT	1970	Bedford TKEL/HCB Angus	Cambridge, Sawston, Manea, Huntingdon	1983
SVE 668K	PHP	1972	ERF/Simon SS50	Cambridge	1983 **(10)**
TJE 485K	WrL	1972	Bedford TKEL/HCB Angus	Wisbech, Linton, St Neots	1986
TJE 486K	WrT	1972	Bedford TKEL/HCB Angus	Swaffham Bulbeck, Soham	1986
WCE 682L	WrL	1973	Bedford TKEL/HCB Angus	Wisbech, Sutton Whittlesey, PVFB	1983
WJE 265L	WrC	1973	Bedford TKM 4×4/Gladwins	Cambridge, Yaxley	1996

(10) Pump Hydraulic Platform.

HUNTINGDONSHIRE & PETERBOROUGH FIRE APPLIANCES 1965–1974

Reg.	Type	Date	Manufacturer	Details	Sold
CEW 112C	WrL	1965	Bedford TJ4/Dennis M	Huntingdon, Kimbolton	1979
CEW 600C	WrC	1965	Bedford RLHZ 4×4/Marshall	Dogsthorpe, Yaxley	
EEW 694C	WrC	1965	Bedford RLHZ 4×4/Marshall	Huntingdon, Yaxley	1986
FEW 883D	WrT	1966	Bedford RLHZH/HCB Angus	Huntingdon, Thorney	
FVE 252D	WrT	1966	Bedford RLHZ/HCB Angus	Dogsthorpe, Whittlesey	1983
GFL 920D	WrT	1966	Bedford RLHZ/HCB Angus	PVFB	
GFL 990D	WrT	1966	Bedford RLHZH/HCB Angus	Ramsey	
HEW 148E	WrT	1967	Bedford RLHZH/HCB Angus	Dogsthorpe, St Ives	
HCE 486F	WrT	1967	Bedford TK/HCB Angus	Dogsthorpe, St Ives	1979
HEW 412F	WrL	1968	Bedford TK/HCB Angus	Dogsthorpe, PVFB, St Neots, Kimbolton	
PFL 78G	WrT	1969	ERF	Dogsthorpe, Chatteris	1986
LEW 516H	WrL	1970	ERF	Huntingdon, Manea	1985
NEW 599J	WrL	1971	Bedford TK/HCB Angus	St Neots, Ramsey, Sawtry	1986
YEG 729J	WrT	1971	Dennis Rolls F48	PVFB	
HEG 700L	WrT	1973	Bedford TKEL/HCB Angus	Huntingdon, Yaxley, Training Centre	Preserved
NFL 603M	WrL	1974	ERF	Huntingdon, St Ives	1985

CAMBRIDGESHIRE FIRE & RESCUE SERVICE FIRE APPLIANCES 1974 ONWARDS

Pumping Appliances

Reg.	Type	Date	Manufacturer	Details	Sold
REG 784M	WrL	1974	Dodge K850/HCB Angus	PVFB, Sutton	
GEB 871N	WrL	1975	Dodge K850/HCB Angus	Dogsthorpe, Papworth	
HEB 513N	WrL	1975	Dodge K850/HCB Angus	Wisbech, Yaxley, Manea	
HEB 514N	WrL	1975	Dodge K850/HCB Angus	Ely	
PVE 832N	WrL	1975	Dodge K850/HCB Angus	Cambridge, Ely, Ramsey	
PVE 833N	WrL	1975	Dodge K850/HCB Angus	Cambridge, Wisbech, Chatteris, PVFB	
LVE 773P	WrL	1975	Dodge K1113/HCB Angus	Cambridge, Huntingdon, Burwell	
LVE 774P	WrL	1975	Dodge K1113/HCB Angus	Cambridge, Ramsey	
LVE 775P	WrL	1975	Dodge K1113/HCB Angus	Dogsthorpe, Cottenham	
LVE 776P	WrL	1975	Dodge K1113/HCB Angus	Stanground, Soham	
NVE 195R	WrL	1977	Dodge K1113/ERF Firefighter	Stanground, Thorney	
NVE 196R	WrL	1977	Dodge K1113/ERF Firefighter	Dogsthorpe, Whittlesey	
NVE 197R	WrL	1977	Dodge K1113/ERF Firefighter	Cambridge, Wisbech, Gamlingay	
NVE 198R	WrL	1977	Dodge K1113/ERF Firefighter	Cambridge, March	
SCE 667S	WrL	1978	Dodge K1113/CFE	St Neots, Swaffham Bulbeck, Soham	1994
SCE 668S	WrL	1978	Dodge K1113/CFE	St Neots, Cambridge, Manea	
SCE 669S	WrL	1978	Dodge K1113/CFE	Cambridge, Wisbech, Littleport	
SCE 670S	WrL	1978	Dodge K1113/CFE	Sawston, St Ives, Burwell	
YCE 219T	WrL	1979	Dodge G1313/HCB Angus	Dogsthorpe, Kimbolton, Thorney	1992
BJE 360V	WrL	1979	Dodge G1313/HCB Angus	Dogsthorpe, Huntingdon, PVFB	1994
BVA 15V	WrL	1980	Bedford TKG/HCB Angus	Cambridge, March, Linton	1994
BVA 16V	WrL	1980	Bedford TKG/HCB Angus	Cambridge, Wisbech, Linton	1993
LEW 625W	WrL	1981	Bedford TKG/CFE	Wisbech, Sawtry	1992
SEG 800X	WrL	1982	Bedford TKG/CMC	St Neots	1994
SEG 806X	WrL	1982	Bedford TKG/CMC	Huntingdon	1993
UEW 462X	WrL	1982	Bedford TKG/HCB Angus	Wisbech, March	1994
UEW 463X	WrL	1982	Bedford TKG/HCB Angus	Ely, Sutton	1996
AEG 691Y	WrL	1983	Dennis RS133/JDC	Dogsthorpe, PVFB	1996
AEG 692Y	WrL	1983	Dennis RS133/JDC	Cambridge, St Ives	1996
AEG 693Y	WrL	1983	Dennis RS133/JDC	Cambridge, Papworth, Manea	1996

Registration	In service	Type	Model	Stations / Locations	Withdrawn
AEG 694Y	1983	WrL	Dennis RS133/JDC	Stanground, Cottenham, Soham, PVFB	1996
A727 MEG	1983	WrL	Dennis RS133/JDC	Wisbech, Ramsey	1997
A728 MEG	1983	WrL	Dennis RS133/JDC	Huntingdon, Ramsey	1996
A729 MEG	1983	WrL	Dennis RS133/JDC	St Neots, St Ives, Fire Cadets	2000
B56 EFL	1985	WrL	Dennis RS135/JDC	Wisbech, Yaxley	1999
B57 EFL	1985	WrL	Dennis RS135/JDC	Sawston, Kimbolton	1998
B58 EFL	1985	WrL	Dennis RS135/JDC	Cambridge, Yaxley	1991 (11)
B59 EFL	1985	WrL	Dennis RS135/JDC	Cambridge, Chatteris	1998
B414 JJE	1984	WrL	Dennis RS135/JDC	Ely, Whittlesey, Fire Safety	
B415 JJE	1984	WrL	Dennis RS135/JDC	Dogsthorpe, Swaffham Bulbeck, Manea	1998
B416 JJE	1984	WrL	Dennis RS135/JDC	Stanground, Sawtry	1997
C103 MEW	1986	WrL	Dennis RS135/JDC	St Neots, Burwell	1998
D146 KVA	1987	WrL	Dennis RS135/JDC	Stanground, Thorney	2001
D746 KVA	1987	WrL	Dennis RS135/JDC	Dogsthorpe, Soham	2001
D747 KVA	1987	WrL	Dennis RS135/JDC	Ely, Littleport	1999
D748 KVA	1987	WrL	Dennis RS135/JDC	Huntingdon, March	1998
D749 KVA	1987	WrL	Dennis RS135/JDC	St Neots, Gamlingay, March	2000
E739 KEG	1988	WrL	Dennis RS135/Fulton & Wylie	Sawston, Linton	2000
E740 KEG	1988	WrL	Dennis RS135/Fulton & Wylie	Huntingdon, Training Centre	1998
E741 KEG	1988	WrL	Dennis RS135/Fulton & Wylie	Cambridge, Soham, Whittlesey, Fire Cadets	
E742KEG	1988	WrL	Dennis RS135/Fulton & Wylie	Cambridge, Cottenham, PVFB	2001
E743 KEG	1988	WrL	Dennis RS135/Fulton & Wylie	Wisbech, PVFB	2000
F808 AAV	1989	WrL	Dennis RS237/JDC	Dogsthorpe, Training Centre	2002
F809 AAV	1989	WrL	Dennis RS237/JDC	Stanground, Ely, Training Centre	2002
F810 AAV	1989	WrL	Dennis RS237/JDC	Ely	2005
F811 AAV	1989	WrL	Dennis RS237/JDC	St Neots, Training Centre	2002
G592 OFL	1990	WrL	Dennis RS237/JDC	Cambridge, Papworth, St Ives, Manea	2005
G593 OFL	1990	WrL	Dennis RS237/JDC	Cambridge, Sawston, Sutton, PVFB	2004
G594 OFL	1990	WrL	Dennis RS237/JDC	Dogsthorpe, Gamlingay, Ramsey	2005
G595 OFL	1990	WrL	Dennis RS237/JDC	Stanground, Cottenham, Ramsey	2005
H491 DFL	1991	WrL	Dennis RS237/JDC	Wisbech, Training Centre, reserve	2005
H492 DFL	1991	WrL	Dennis RS237/JDC	Huntingdon, Sawston, reserve	2005
H493 DFL	1991	WrL	Dennis RS237/JDC	St Neots, Ely, reserve	
J988 TEG	1992	WrL	Dennis RS237/JDC	Cambridge, Huntingdon, reserve	
J989 TEG	1992	WrL	Dennis RS237/JDC	Dogsthorpe, Wisbech, Soham	

Registration	Type	Year	Chassis	Location
J990 TEG	WrL	1992	Dennis RS237/JDC	Cambridge, St Neots, reserve
K681 BEW	WrL	1992	Dennis RS237/JDC	Stanground, S. Ives
K682 BEW	WrL	1992	Dennis RS237/JDC	Huntingdon, Swaffham Bulbeck, St Ives
L577 PFL	WrL	1993	Dennis RS237/JDC	St Neots, Training Centre, Sawtry, Manea
L578 PFL	WrL	1993	Dennis RS237/JDC	Ely, Sawston, Littleport
L723 NAV	WrL	1993	Dennis RS237/JDC	Wisbech, Gamlingay, March, Linton, reserve
M846 GEG	WrL	1995	Dennis RS241/JDC	Cambridge, Ely, Soham, Burwell
M847 GEG	WrL	1995	Dennis RS241/JDC	Cambridge, Papworth, March, Thorney, Ramsey
M848 GEG	WrL	1995	Dennis RS241/JDC	Dogsthorpe, Huntingdon, Cottenham, Yaxley, Ramsey
N489 SAV	WrL	1996	Dennis TSD203 Sabre/JDC	Cambridge, St Neots, Chatteris
N490 SAV	WrL	1996	Dennis TSD203 Sabre/JDC	Cambridge, Ely, Swaffham Bulbeck
N491 SAV	WrL	1996	Dennis TSD203 Sabre/JDC	Stanground, Wisbech. Kimbolton, Yaxley
N492 SAV	WrL	1996	Dennis TSD203 Sabre/JDC	Dogsthorpe, Huntingdon, Training Centre
P150 GFL	WrL	1996	Dennis TSD203 Sabre/JDC	Stanground, Wisbech, PVFB
P151 GFL	WrL	1996	Dennis TSD203 Sabre/JDC	Dogsthorpe, Huntingdon, Soham
P152 GFL	WrL	1996	Dennis TSD203 Sabre/JDC	Cambridge, Ely, Papworth
P153 GFL	WrL	1996	Dennis TSD203 Sabre/JDC	Cambridge, St Neots, Cottenham, Huntingdon
R862 EFL	WrL	1997	Dennis TSD203 Sabre/JDC	Cambridge, Ely, March
R863 EFL	WrL	1997	Dennis TSD203 Sabre/JDC	Dogsthorpe, St Neots, Gamlingay
R864 EFL	WrL	1997	Dennis TSD203 Sabre/JDC	Stanground, Huntingdon, Sawston, Ramsey
R865 EFL	WrL	1997	Dennis TSD203 Sabre/JDC	Cambridge, Training Centre, March
S47 BCE	WrL	1999	Dennis TSD203 Sabre/JDC	Dogsthorpe, Huntingdon, Ely, Thorney
S48 BCE	WrL	1999	Dennis TSD203 Sabre/JDC	Stanground, St Neots, Sutton
S49 BCE	WrL	1999	Dennis TSD203 Sabre/JDC	Cambridge, Whittlesey
T905 WVA	WrL	1999	Dennis TSD203 Sabre/JDC	Cambridge, St Neots, Sawtry
T906 WVA	WrL	1999	Dennis TSD203 Sabre/JDC	Stanground, Wisbech, Linton
T907 WVA	WrL	1999	Dennis TSD203 Sabre/JDC	Dogsthorpe, Huntingdon, Training Centre
Y991 WFL	WrL	2001	Scania P94D-260/JDC	Cambridge, Ely
Y992 WFL	WrL	2001	Scania P94D-260/JDC	Dogsthorpe, Wisbech
Y993 WFL	WrL	2001	Scania P94D-260/JDC	Stanground, St Neots
AF02 XTJ	WrL	2002	Scania P94D-260/JDC	Cambridge, Kimbolton
AF02 XTK	WrL	2002	Scania P94D-260/JDC	Huntingdon, St Ives

Registration	Type	Model	Station	Year
AF02 XTL	WrL	Scania P94D-260/JDC	Wisbech	2002
AE03 OUP	WrL	Scania P94D-260/JDC	Cambridge, Cottenham	2003
AE03 OUS	WrL	Scania P94D-260/JDC	Stanground, Ely	2003
AE03 OUU	WrL	Scania P94D-260/JDC	Dogsthorpe, Sawston	2003
KX53 FJV	WrL	Scania P94D-260/Emergency One	Stanground, St Neots	2004
KX53 FJY	WrL	Scania P94D-260/Emergency One	Cambridge	2004
KX53 FJZ	WrL	Scania P94D-260/Emergency One	Huntingdon	2004
KP54 CWX	WrL	Scania P94D-260/Emergency One	Stanground	2005
KP54 CWY	WrL	Scania P94D-260/Emergency One	Cambridge	2005
KP54 CWZ	WrL	Scania P94D-260/Emergency One	Dogsthorpe	2005

(11) Destroyed in field fire.

Specialist Appliances

Registration	Type	Model	Station	Year	Year
WVE 742T	TL	Shelvoke & Drewry/Benson/Metz	Cambridge	1979	1983 (12)
BVA 9V	RT	Stonefield P6000 6×4/CMC	Dogsthorpe	1980	1988
DEB 896V	RT	Stonefield P6000 6×4/CMC	Cambridge, Wisbech	1980	1989
UEW 460X	RT/CU	Bedford TKG/CMC	Huntingdon	1982	1989
A308 VEG	TL	Iveco 192D14/Carmichael/Magirus	Dogsthorpe	1984	1998
A621 SEW	TL	Iveco 192D14/Carmichael/Magirus	Cambridge	1984	1999
B216 NVT	RT	GMC C20NC/Woodway	Cambridge	1984	1985 (13)
B868 FEG	WrC	Bedford TKM 4×4/Carmichael	Wisbech, Huntingdon	1985	1994
C630 LFL	RT	GMC K20/Woodway	Cambridge	1985	1994
C643 KCE	CIU	Ford Transit	St Neots	1986	1994
D750 KVA	WrC	Bedford TKM 4×4/JDC	Cambridge, Huntingdon, Wisbech, Yaxley	1987	2002
D940 EEW	RT	GMC K30FC/Woodway	Dogsthorpe	1988	1989 (14)
F611 BAV	PM	Volvo FL614/Multilift	Huntingdon	1989	1999
F612 BAV	PM, HSRU	Volvo FL614/Multilift	Huntingdon, 1992 converted to HSRU, St Neots	1989	2004
	Pod, ICCU	Fulton & Wylie	Huntingdon	1989	1997
	Pod, SRU	Fulton & Wylie	Huntingdon	1989	1991 (15)
H151 JFL	SRU	Mercedes 1120AF 4×4/Rosenbauer	Huntingdon	1991	2001 (15)
H410 CEW	RT	Mercedes 811D/Carmichael	Dogsthorpe	1991	1999
J359 SEW	FCU	Land Rover Defender	Dogsthorpe	1992	2005 (16)

Reg	Code	Make/Model	Year	Location	Note
L351 PFL	RDCU	Mercedes 1124AF/Angloco	1993	Cambridge, reserve	(17)
L140 VCE	WFoU	Mercedes 2531 6×4/Carmichael/Dennis Eagle	1994	Huntingdon	
L452 TFL	OSU	Mercedes 814D/Gladwin	1994	Huntingdon, March	
R615 TAV	ICU	Mercedes 817/Excalibur	1997	Huntingdon	
T837 RFL	TL	MAN M2000/Magirus/GB Fire	1999	Dogsthorpe	
T838 RFL	RV	MAN L2000/JDC	1999	Dogsthorpe	
T839 RFL	CFSV	MAN L2000/JDC	1999	Community Fire Safety	2005 (18)
V879 UEW	TL	MAN M2000/Magirus/GB Fire	2000	Cambridge	
Y724 WVA	RV	MAN L2000/JDC	2001	Huntingdon	
AF51 DWL	RV	MAN L2000/JDC	2002	Cambridge	
AF52 VMM	WrC	MAN LE280B 4×4/Massey Tankers	2003	Yaxley	
DG53 FZL	IRU	MAN TGA 6×2/Marshalls SV	2004	Stanground	
	FLT	Moffat Mounty	2004	Stanground	(19)
AE04 FVH	HMU	Mercedes Vario 814D/Emergency One	2004	St Neots	
AE05 GYY	CFSV	Iveco Van	2005	Community Fire Safety	(18)
WX54 VMJ	HVPU	MAN TGA 6×2/Marshalls SV/Hydrant Fire System Pump	2006	Huntingdon	

(12) Written off following RTA.
(13) Written off following RTA.
(14) Destroyed in explosion, Peterborough.
(15) Special Rescue Unit.
(16) Forward Control Unit.
(17) Rescue Damage Control Unit.
(18) Community Fire Safety Vehicle.
(19) Fork Lift Truck carried on IRU.

**RULES AND REGULATIONS
OF THE ST NEOTS
VOLUNTEER FIRE BRIGADE**

1. The Brigade shall be called 'THE ST NEOTS VOLUNTEER FIRE BRIGADE', and shall consist of a Captain, 1st and 2nd Lieutenants, an Engineer, Secretary and Treasurer, Ten Firemen and Two Call Boys.

2. The Brigade Uniform shall consist of Trousers, Tunic, Helmet, Boots and Belt with Axe, Spanner and Life Line. No person can be recognised at any Drill as a member of the Brigade unless in uniform and no Member shall appear in uniform unless on duty, or by permission of the Captain.

3. The business of the Brigade to be conducted by the whole Brigade, seven Members to form a quorum.

4. There shall be an Annual General Meeting of the Brigade in January in each year, to receive statement of accounts and consider the appointment of Officers and any other business which shall be brought forward; every other meeting of the Brigade shall be a Special Meeting and shall be called by the Secretary by three days notice to all Members.

5. The Engineer of the Brigade is a servant of the St Neots Urban District Council and shall be subject to these rules.

6. That the Brigade shall Drill at least twice a month, or more frequently if the Officers shall deem it desirable. Any Member attending less than twelve Drills in the year (unless prevented by illness or by permission of the Captain, fires not to count as Drills) shall be struck off the roll.

7. The Brigade shall be under the management of the Captain, and his absence, of the Senior Officer present, who shall be deemed the Officer-in-Charge, and any Member acting upon orders received from any other person, or disregarding the orders of the Captain or Officer-in-Charge, or using improper language or otherwise misbehaving himself whilst in the uniform of the Brigade, or damaging the property in charge of the Brigade, or for any other offence, shall be reported to the Committee.

8. That Members so reported shall be liable to expulsion from the Brigade.

9. At a Fire, the Captain, when Manual is used, shall select his pumpers, and affix to the arm of each man so selected a badge. The badge must be delivered up to the Secretary, and no man will under any circumstances be remunerated except on production of the badge.

10. Any member wishing to leave the Brigade shall give 28 days' notice in writing to the Secretary, and at the expiration of that time he shall send in his uniform. Any member leaving the town is at once to send in his uniform to the Secretary.

11. A Special Meeting of the Brigade shall be called on the requisition of any three Members addressed to the Captain and Secretary, stating the purpose of such Meeting, and the Secretary shall thereupon give notice thereof.

12. In cases of vacancies occurring in the Brigade, candidates must, at a meeting called in the usual way, be proposed and seconded by two Members of the Brigade, and be elected by ballot, subject, however, in all cases to the Regulations hereinafter set forth.

13. Subject to the foregoing Regulations, all monies received for attending Fires or otherwise shall be distributed amongst the various persons entitled thereto by the Secretary and Treasurer, as directed by the Captain, and they shall have power to deduct thereout a sum not exceeding 2/- from each £1 from the Captain, and 1/- from each Member, of the whole of such monies, which shall become part of the Brigade Funds.

14. The following Charges shall be made by the Brigade:-

Steamer	£5 5s. 0d.	per day
Subsequent days	£2 2s. 0d.	,,
Manual	£2 2s. 0d.	,,
Captain, first two hours	4s. 0d.	per hour
Captain, afterwards	2s. 0d.	,,
Other Members, first two hours	2s. 0d.	,,
Other Members, afterwards	1s. 6d.	,,
Call Messengers	2s. 6d.	per call
Supernumeraries	6d.	per hour

15. The St Neots Urban District Council have agreed to make an Annual Allowance to the Brigade, the same to be distributed by the Secretary and Treasurer as directed by the Captain amongst the Members of the Brigade as follows:-

Captain	£2 0s. 0d.
First Lieutenant	£1 0s. 0d.
Second Lieutenant	£1 0s. 0d.
Secretary	£1 0s. 0d.
Treasurer	£1 0s. 0d.
Each Fireman	£1 0s. 0d.

Any Member who shall commit any breach of these Rules or infringe the Regulations aforesaid, shall forewith forfeit his share in the Annual Allowance, and the same shall not be payable by the Council to the Brigade or any Member thereof.

16. That the Secretary shall enter in proper books, to be kept for the purpose, minutes of all business done, and shall conduct the correspondence of the Brigade, and produce the same at every Meeting for the inspection of the Members.

17. That the Treasurer shall keep an account of all Receipts and Payments, and all payments shall by cheque, signed by the Secretary and the Treasurer, after being passed at any Meeting of the Brigade.

18. That two Honorary Auditors shall be appointed, who shall examine and verify the Accounts to be presented at the Annual Meeting.

19. That all complaints, whether by the Members of the Brigade or the Public, shall be investigated by the Officers, who shall have full power to decide all matters.

20. That a List of all Members, with their addresses, shall be sent to the Members of the Police Force, who are requested to call the Members upon an alarm of Fire.

21. These Rules of the Fire Brigade shall be subscribed by every Member of the Brigade and also the Engineer, as approving and agreeing thereto.

Sealed by the Council and signed by the other persons hereinafter referred to this 7th day of December 1905.

The following signatures are appended:-

Frank Nichols (Capt.)
Malcolm McNish (1st Lieut.)
Thomas Williamson (2nd Lieut.)
Ernest Lee (Engineer)
Samuel H. Clarabut (Hon. Sec.)
Robert T. Clisby (Hon. Treasurer)
Herbert Pate
Alfred Pearson (Chairman – Fire Brigade Committee of the U.D.C.)
Frederick Squires
Wilfred Gilbert
George Last
Thomas Haynes
Alfred Ireland (Clerk to the St Neots Council)
Percy Williamson
John Knight
Albert Cook
Frank Lovett

GLOSSARY

GENERAL

AFA – Automatic fire alarm which sends a message to the local control centre.

Arson – Wilfully or maliciously setting fire to property.

Auxiliary Fire Service (AFS) – Auxiliary Fire Service, established in 1937 to recruit and train additional firemen and women in preparation for the outbreak of the Second World War and absorbed into the NFS in 1941. Reformed in 1949 and finally disbanded in 1968.

BA – Breathing Apparatus, collective term for a variety of compressed air cylinders worn with face masks to enable firemen to work in thick smoke or poisonous gases.

Hosereel – A line of small diameter hose (180 feet), coiled on a drum ready for immediate use.

Hydrant – Water supply point from mains found in every street, usually under the surface of the pavement and marked on an adjacent wall by a yellow plate.

Informative Message – Details of an incident, not yet under control, giving details advising Control Staff and oncoming appliances.

Jet – A hose line.

Make–up – An incident in which the initial attendance of appliances is insufficient and more resources are required.

Monitor – A piece of equipment capable of supplying a large quantity of water. Can be either portable (ground monitor) or fixed to the top of a turntable ladder or hydraulic platform.

National Fire Service (NFS) – Formed in 1941 to provide the whole country with a unified Fire Service. Disbanded in 1948.

On the run – An expression originating in Victorian times when the fire engine stood ready for action on a sloping section of floor designed to assist the initial pull of the horses. Today 'on the run' is used when ready for action.

Open Water – A water supply not coming from a water mains, e.g. pond, river etc.

Persons reported – Priority message to indicate that persons are reported to be trapped in a fire.

Shout – An emergency call. This term originated in Victorian times when horse drawn appliances did not have any form of warning device apart from the crew shouting at passers by to clear the way, hence on 'a shout'.

Smoke Issuing – Self explanatory Fire Service description of smoke seen coming from a building.

Special Service Call – A non–fire emergency.

215

Stop Message – A message sent to fire control, normally by radio to indicate that an incident is under control and that no further assistance is required.

Turn out – Mobilise to an emergency call.

Watch room – Nerve centre of a fire station, where the log book is kept and where emergency calls are received.

APPLIANCES

Chemical Incident Unit (CIU) – Appliances carrying protective suits and specialist equipment to deal with chemical and other hazardous incidents.

Control Unit (CU) or Incident Control Unit (ICU) – Mobile control room containing radios, maps etc. used by senior officers to control larger incidents.

Emergency Tender (ET) – A special appliance carrying a large variety of tools and rescue equipment, basically a mobile workshop.

Fire Victim Support Unit (FVSU) – A vehicle based on a motor home, manned by Red Cross volunteers, which attends incidents, in particular when families have been forced out of their homes by fire or flooding. Normally based at a Fire Station.

Forward Control Unit (FCU) – Four wheeled drive vehicle used for accessing incidents where the Incident Control Unit cannot reach.

Hazardous Substances Rescue Unit (HSRU) or Hazardous Materials Unit (HMU) – Same as a Chemical Incident Unit but re-named to show the broader role carried out.

Incident Response Unit (IRU) – Appliance supplied by Central Government as part of the 'New Dimensions' project. Carries equipment to deal with large scale biological and chemical attacks.

Operational Support Unit (OSU) – Appliance carrying out any number of roles. In Cambridgeshire the OSU combines the roles of a Mobile Canteen and Breathing Apparatus Support Unit.

Pod – Container type unit built to be loaded onto a Prime Mover. In Cambridgeshire they consisted of an Incident Control Unit, Ops Support Unit and Special Rescue Unit.

Prime Mover (PM) – Appliance consisting of a crew cab and an open chassis onto which various pods can be loaded.

Pump (P) – Pumping appliance carrying a 30 feet ladder but with a limited water capacity. Also a generic term for any fire appliance carrying a crew of between four and six, breathing apparatus, ladders and other firefighting and rescue gear and capable of pumping water.

Pump Escape (PE) – Pumping appliance carrying a 50 feet wheeled escape. In modern days it has been replaced by the Water Tender Ladder.

Rescue Tender (RT) or Rescue Vehicle (RV) – A special appliance carrying a large variety of tools and rescue equipment.

Special Appliance – A non-pumping fire engine, e.g. Turntable Ladder, Rescue Tender etc.

Trailer Pump – Pumps mainly used during the Second World War carried on a two wheeled trailer and towed behind a variety of vehicles.

Turntable Ladder (TL) – An appliance fitted with a 100 feet extending ladder capable of rotating around 360 degrees.

Water Carrier (WrC) – A special appliance capable of carrying a large quantity of water.

Water/Foam Unit (WFoU) – A special appliance capable of carrying large quantities of water and/or foam.

Water Tender (WrT) – Pumping appliance carrying a 35 feet extension ladder and 1,800 litres of water.

Water Tender Ladder (WrL) – As above but carrying a 45 feet extension ladder.

DUTY SYSTEMS

Wholetime – A system which maintains 24-hour cover on fire stations. There are four watches (Red, White, Blue and Green). One watch working days (09.00 to 18.00), one working nights (18.00 to 09.00) with two watches off duty. The system covers an eight-day period; two days on duty, two nights on duty and four days off.

Day Manning – A system which uses full-time firefighters who man the appliance(s) during the daytime but respond to alerter callout from their homes close to the fire station at night.

Alternate Manning – A system where a crew is allocated to more than one appliance and man whichever one is required for a particular incident.

Retained – Stations in smaller towns or villages where the crew is made up of part-time firefighters who follow their normal jobs and respond from work or home in response to an alerter call.

RANKS IN THE FIRE SERVICE

Firefighter – A crew member of a fire appliance.

Leading Firefighter – In charge of a fire appliance.

Sub Officer – In charge of a watch (shift) and a fire appliance.

Station Officer – In charge of a fire station.

Assistant Divisional Officer – In charge of a larger fire station/several stations.

Divisional Officer – In charge of a group of fire stations (a division).

Senior Divisional Officer – In charge of a large division or support section.

Assistant Chief Officer – Based at headquarters and responsible for a range of support sections.

Deputy Chief Fire Officer – Similar to ACO but deputises for CFO.

Chief Fire Officer – In command of the brigade and responsible to the fire authority.

BIBLIOGRAPHY

A Celebration of the work of Peterborough Volunteer Fire Brigade 1884–1994 – *Neil Wallington.*

A Centenary History of the Peterborough Volunteer Fire Brigade (1884–1984) – 'Ready & Willing' – *Richard Hillier.*

Cambridge – *F. A. Reeve.*

Golden Memories of Fire Brigades in Cambridgeshire – *Gordon Townsend.*

History of a Huntingdonshire Town – *C. F. Tebbutt.*

The Book of Huntingdon – *Christopher Dunn.*

Cambridgeshire Fire Brigade – Annual Reports (various).

Cambridgeshire Fire Brigade – Committee Minutes (various).

Cambridgeshire Fire & Rescue Service – Annual Reports (various).

Fire Cover – The Journal of The Fire Brigade Society (various).

History of the Huntingdon and Peterborough County Fire Service 1965–1974.

Huntingdonshire County Fire Service – Incident Log Books (various).

Kimbolton Fire Station – Incident Log Books (various).

Soke of Peterborough Fire Brigade – Incident Log Books (various).

St Neots Volunteer Fire Brigade Minutes and Fire Reports 1909–1934.

St Neots Urban District Fire Brigade Minutes and Fire Reports 1934–1941.

St Neots Urban District Fire Brigade Fire Reports 1934–1941.

St Neots Fire Station – Incident Log Books (various).